D0914581

A WOMAN'S JOURNEY
TO THE NORTH POLE

Matty L. McNair

Printed and bound in Canada.

Canadian cataloguing in publication data

McNair, Matty L.
On thin ice: a woman's journey to the North Pole

ISBN 0-9685343-0-9

1. Women's Polar Relay Expedition. 2. McNair, Matty L. – Journeys – North Pole. 3. Martin, Denise, 1966- – Journeys – North Pole. 4. Canada, Northern – Description and travel. 5. North Pole – Description and travel. 6. Cross-country skiing – Canada, Northern. I. Title.

G585.M35A3 1999   910'.9163'2   C99-900600-2

Published by NorthWinds, PO Box 820, Iqaluit NT Canada X0A 0H0

For ordering information, please contact:

NorthWinds Arctic Adventures
PO Box 820
Iqaluit, NT Canada X0A 0H0
Tel.: 867-979-0551, 1-800-549-0551
Fax: 867-979-0573
e-mail: plandry@nunanet.com

Cover photo: Matty McNair

Back cover photo: Denise Martin

Contents

Foreword

By Matty McNair

Before my feet had recovered from the journey to the top of the world, I was inundated with people asking if I would write a book. They had read many heroic tales of men's attempts to conquer the Arctic and wanted to know how a small woman in her late 40s had successfully led a group of inexperienced women to the Geographic North Pole. I was encouraged by their enthusiasm—that they wished to read of a journey that was not about glorious failures such as Franklin's quest for the Northwest Passage or Scott's expedition to the South Pole.

I must admit that I am more at home on the ice than writing at a computer. It has taken me longer to write my journal into book form than it took to trudge to the North Pole.

I have strived to maintain the essence of my original journal that I so diligently wrote during the expedition. To enhance its readability and save you from tedious boredom, I have deleted repetitive entries such as, "It was another long hard day." (Believe me there were a lot of those!) I have also expanded entries such as, "Tonight I told the story of Sedna," and filled in the story of the Inuit sea goddess.

I value integrity and honesty and so it is important to me that this book reflect the truth of my experience. I have a strong dislike for authors that exaggerate, making a

-20° C into a -45° C day or distort the truth to make a more suspenseful, sellable book. I have learned that truth is fluid and not easily defined. How I interpreted events on the polar ice is not necessarily how I view them now. The frustrations that overwhelmed me at the time, like a burnt dinner, now seem so trivial. However laughable these feelings seem to me now, I have related them because, at the time, that was how I felt. I also expect that my truth or perspective differs slightly from that of the other women on the relay.

This book is an account of the journey to the North Pole as I experienced it. It is about my struggle to keep in balance the focus for the drive towards "The Big Nail" with my belief that the key to success is in the style in which the journey is lived. It is about sharing the leadership with Denise Martin and the trust, respect and friendship that evolved. And it is about the incredible journey that I shared with 20 amazing women who had the courage, the boldness, and the tenacity to succeed against great odds.

Matty McNair
March 1999, Iqaluit

Foreword

By Denise Martin

In mid-August of 1996 I received a telephone call from Matty. She asked me "Do you want to lead a trip to the North Pole with me?" Without hesitation I responded "Yes, of course."

I had known Matty for years and considered her a mentor and role model. I valued her opinions and trusted her judgment. Matty's leadership style is one that empowers individuals and develops trust amongst the team members. What I discovered on the ice was that these skills were key ingredients that brought magic to our journey and success in reaching our goal.

For me, a day does not go by when I do not reflect on my journey to the North Pole. I had the time of my life and find myself reminiscing about silly (and serious) incidents we found ourselves in. I often think of the women with fondness, the friendships I made and the incredible wonder and beauty of life on the ice. The simplicity of life and the focus on core values made the expedition more than just a physical feat. The expedition was a historical achievement and I am proud to be part of that. However, the success was in how we worked together and gained strength from one another.

To have shared this expedition with my friend Matty made the experience even richer. I am proud to have completed this journey with such an exceptional person and to have skied beside her for the 416 nautical miles to North Pole.

Thank you Matty.

Denise Martin
March 1999, Saskatoon

Preparations

FEB. 20, 1997, IQALUIT, NUNAVUT, CANADA

For weeks I've been hoping for a flash of inspiration to start my journal.

Yet now that I've stolen the time from my other pressing responsibilities, I am unable to find the inspirational opening lines that this grand expedition deserves. So, I fall back on my motto: "When stuck, fear not failure, push onward." (Here goes...)

I am preparing to lead the first women's expedition to the Geographic North Pole. (Weak, but it's a start. I'll try again...)

I have taken on the enormous responsibility of guiding 20 "ordinary British women" to fulfill their dream of participating in a relay expedition to the North Pole. (More informative, but not very dramatic, how about...)

The first-ever women's expedition to the North Pole is about to launch its attack into the harshest environment on earth, the Polar Ice Cap. Will we make history and put the "Great" back into Britain; or will this be just another British "glorious failure" like the last nine British North Pole attempts? (A bit too British, and too sensational.)

I am about to begin a long, long journey that will challenge my physical and mental endurance. My responsibilities are clear: I've been hired to safely lead five teams of

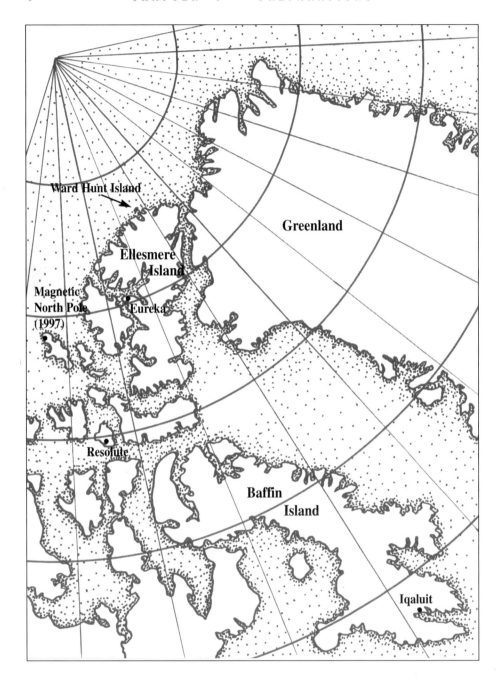

four women from the northern tip of Ellesmere Island to the top of the world, the North Pole! (Well, not exceptional but better.)

I will start at the beginning because I am a person who likes progressive order. In the spring of 1996, my husband and business partner, Paul Landry, was at a travel show in London, England, marketing our adventure travel company, NorthWinds Arctic Adventures, when he met Pen Hadow. Pen was starting the Polar Travel Company and had been approached by Caroline Hamilton to help her organize a women's relay expedition to the North Pole. Pen was looking for a Canadian adventure company to assist him with the organization of the expedition. He was also looking for a woman to lead the expedition.

Upon hearing of Pen's plan, Paul boldly stated, "There is only one woman who can get your team safely to the North Pole: Matty McNair." To put a wrinkle in time, here I am, on my way to the North Pole. Tomorrow I must say good-bye to my family—Paul, Eric (age 12) and Sarah (age 10), fly to Resolute via Yellowknife, and spend the next three weeks in final preparations.

FEB. 21, ON FLIGHT TO YELLOWKNIFE, NORTHWEST TERRITORIES, CANADA

Saying good-bye at the airport was difficult. I will miss my family and all the support they've given me over the last several months of North Pole preparations. How long will it be until I see them again? How will Eric and Sarah cope with my long absence? Will Paul be okay with the added responsibilities caused by my departure? Who will remember to water my plants? I don't feel ready to say good-bye or ready to leap into the expedition. Self doubts, possibly caused by fear of failure, whirl through my mind.

Being strapped into my seat on the flight to Yellowknife allows me time to reflect and record in my journal my involvement with the expedition over the last six months. Pen and I exchanged numerous faxes over the summer months, sharing our views and opinions on my role as leader, the selection of women, training, itinerary, safety management on the ice, equipment, clothing, food and so on. By September, Paul and I were ready to commit to the expedition, but first there were a number of issues that had to be resolved.

First, was this an all-women's expedition? Pen and Caroline assumed that Pen would be on the expedition for some or all of the relay legs. I disagreed. If this was to be a women's expedition, should it not have all women leaders? I pointed out that they were selling this expedition to the media as "The Women's Polar Relay." It would no longer be a women's expedition the moment a man joined the team. If being the first women's expedition to attempt the North Pole was important, we should look for another woman leader to work with me.

My second concern was the selection of an assistant leader. I wanted the final word in choosing who I would work with. My first choice was Denise Martin. I had known Denise for many years. We met at the Canadian Outward Bound Wilderness School in Northern Ontario, and Denise had worked with me for three years, when I was the program manager for the Arctic Outward Bound programs. Denise is 30, a strong skier, and very experienced at managing groups in a cold environment. More importantly, she is a tough cookie, strong as an ox and a no-bullshit person with compassion. Denise and I had been through rough spots in our past working relationship; we are both strong leaders. We know each other's strengths and vulnerabilities and have developed a working relationship based on trust and respect. At the end of September, I tracked down Denise in Whitehorse, in the Yukon Territory. "Denise, do you want to assist me with a women's expedition to the North Pole?" Denise didn't hesitate for a second, "Sure! When do we leave?" Getting Denise on-board was a major step in setting the stage for success.

My third issue was "all or nothing." Pen and Caroline did not want the leaders to travel the entire distance from Ellesmere Island to the Pole. They were worried that it might steal the spotlight from the 20 British women who were only doing one relay leg. In the first contract Pen sent me, he had Denise and me leading the first four sections and was going to pull us out for the final leg to the North Pole. I made it very clear to him that I was not going to work my ass off during the coldest and most difficult part of the expedition only to have someone else escort the expedition on the final leg. No, Denise and I were going the whole way or not at all.

The fourth concern was that I insisted on having input into clothing, equipment and expedition food. I was not prepared to take responsibility for the life and well-being of clients without control of safety-related decisions regarding the clothing and equipment we would use on the ice, and the food we would eat.

Resolving these differences took many more faxes and telephone calls. The contract was re-drafted many times. It got so complicated that Paul and I turned to our good friend, Paul Crawley, a lawyer, to help us out with the contract negotiations throughout the fall.

Then there were the many months of wondering if the expedition was going to reach its fund-raising target of $600,000 Cdn. This left Denise and me swinging back and forth between getting emotionally primed and our bodies into shape and not wanting to set our hopes, hearts and plans on a dream that was not going to happen. September slid by, the cut-off date was pushed back to October, then November... then December. By Christmas my gut was in knots. The funds raised to date could not be spent until the final goal was reached. This meant that no equipment or clothing could be purchased and tested during the fall months. I began to feel that there was insufficient time to attend to all the critical details.

On January 3, I sent a fax to Pen to inform him that I would not lead the expedition. I still have that letter:

There are only eight weeks left before the first team flies into Ward Hunt. Pen, we are not prepared:

1. We have yet to agree on a clothing and equipment list, let alone begun testing, evaluating, purchasing or making necessary modifications.
2. We have yet to agree on a menu, including meals, calorie content and weight.
3. We have yet to agree on an itinerary, a start date, how long each team is on the ice, how much weight each person is pulling, the expected daily mileage.
4. We have yet to review and agree on a training schedule.
5. The "guide" contract is not finalized.

With eight weeks to go, we should be in the final stages of our preparations. The reality, as I see it, is that we've hardly begun preparations!

I recommended that we postpone the expedition to the following year. I was not ready to assume a leadership position for an expedition that placed clients in danger due to poor planning. Nor did I want to risk my reputation on an expedition that was setting itself up for failure. I was determined not to take these inexperienced women into one of the harshest and most remote environments on earth without proper preparations. The 1996 Everest disaster, where paying clients and guides lost their lives, was all too fresh in my mind. After sending that fax, I had the best night's sleep I had had in months.

The next day Pen called me. The 20 women had committed to contributing $3,000.00 each and the expedition had now reached its fund-raising goal. We had a long talk. He acknowledged that the expedition was behind schedule in planning, preparation and logistics and promised to devote more time and energy to this now that funding was in place. He had hired a staff person who would devote all his time to logistical details. If I would reconsider, he and Caroline would fly to Iqaluit the next weekend, bringing a new contract that gave me the absolute final word on all decisions pertaining to safety on the ice and a strong voice in the final selection of equipment, clothing and food. They would also bring samples of clothing, equipment and food with them.

I had a long talk with Paul and Denise that night and in the end decided to give Pen and Caroline a chance to prove that things were not as bad as I perceived them. I promised to make my final decision before they left Iqaluit.

Pen and Caroline flew to Iqaluit and NorthWinds paid for Denise to fly over from Whitehorse. We sat through many long discussions. I explained again and again that I was not about to take responsibility for the lives of 20 women without proper planning and preparations. I would not go onto the ice until I felt confident that all details pertaining to safety, training, communication, base support team, equipment, clothing and food were looked after. Plus, I wanted a voice in dealing with these issues. Pen had a hard time with my position on this matter. He wanted to hire me as a guide or Sherpa, not as a leader. I worried that this difference in perspective on my role would become an ongoing problem in our working relationship. Both Pen and Caroline saw themselves as the leaders, not the coordinators, of the expedition. Yet Caroline has zero expedition or arctic experience and Pen's polar experience is very limited: two solo attempts on the Pole. On his first try he stopped at The Big Lead (about 50 kilometers) and on his second attempt he returned after he broke a ski on his second day.

By Sunday, they had instilled in me the confidence I had lost in their ability to manage this project. Promises were made, the contract signed and I spent the next four weeks ordering and purchasing $74,000.00 worth of equipment, clothing and food. (This reflected about 90% of the equipment, 25% of the clothing, and 60% of the food.) I revised the itinerary, designed a preliminary training schedule, researched communications systems and trained three to four hours per day on Frobisher Bay, pulling a pulk loaded with 55 kilograms of dog food.

In the weeks that followed, as the stress mounted, I wondered why I had changed my mind. In part it was encouragement from Paul, Eric and Sarah. They believed in me and wanted to see me attain the "Top of the World." I didn't want to let them down. Also, I must confess, I can't resist a shining challenge where the odds are against me. Do I have the physical and mental drive that it takes, when so many before me have failed? No one has attempted to lead a group of inexperienced clients from Ward Hunt Island...can I? Such challenges pull out the best in me.

The "fasten seat belt" sign just went on. We are starting our descent to Yellowknife. I look forward to seeing Denise.

FEB. 22, RESOLUTE, NUNAVUT, CANADA

Denise and I flew to Resolute this morning. Pen was suppose to be on the plane but, upon arrival in Resolute, we were told that he fell asleep at the Edmonton airport and missed his flight! The next flight is not until Feb. 25, only a few days before the first relay team arrives. This is unfortunate as it will allow little time to develop a cohesive support team.

Denise and I were met at the airport by Geoff Somers and Michael Ewart-Smith. Geoff Somers is in charge of training the relay teams in Resolute. He has impressive experience in the Antarctic. After a couple of years with the British Antarctic Survey, he returned with Will Steger to complete the first crossing of the Antarctic continent by ski and dog sled. Last year, he was in Resolute leading a trip to the Magnetic North Pole. Mike Ewart-Smith came on board in January to pull together the logistics and keep the finances in balance. A competent small business executive, passionate about racing yachts, he is new to organizing arctic expeditions. Onto his shoulders falls the responsibility of fulfilling promises made by Pen, such as "Anything you need, just ask Mike and he'll get it."

Resolute is situated on a desolate and wind-swept shore line and consists of an airport base connected by a five-kilometer road to the small Inuit village on the bay. When you get off the plane you walk into the small airport terminal and gift shop. Beyond that are numerous warehouses, hangars, maintenance buildings and the Narwhal Hotel. The town of Resolute is a typical northern community with a Northern Store (formerly the Hudson Bay Company), church, school, nursing station, town offices, power generating station, and about 45 small homes.

Our pre-arranged living accommodation fell through. To compensate, Mike and Geoff worked wonders to turn an old storage shed into the Women's Polar Relay Expedition Headquarters. They put up plywood walls to section off an office, workshop, bunk room and shelves for equipment and food and affectionately dubbed it "The Rookery." The name refers to penguin colonies, called rookeries. McVitie's Penguins, makers of Penguin biscuits, are the Gold Sponsor for this expedition (does not matter that penguins actually live in Antarctica and not here in the Arctic!).

MARCH 1, RESOLUTE, NUNAVUT, CANADA

The first team of women flew in this evening. The team looked grand when they stepped off the plane, all dressed in red expedition parkas, covered with an impressive number of sponsorship badges. They greeted Pen, Michael and Geoff with exuberance, sharing news from home and asking questions faster than they could be answered. Denise and I introduced ourselves. It is obvious that we are not yet part of this group. They have gotten to know each other through the selection weekends, fund-raising and training together. Denise and I are clearly the outsiders, an odd position. Usually leaders are the nucleus of a group. The first phase of the group-forming process, with pre-designated leader(s), is that group members first confirm their relationship to the leader(s). Denise and I are accustomed to working with Outward Bound groups that think we are the Goddesses of the Wilderness. So this is different. It will be up to us to gain their recognition, trust and respect.

It is interesting to reflect back on how the women became involved with this expedition. Over the radio, Caroline invited "ordinary women" to join her. Over 200 women applied. A selection weekend was organized for all 200 applicants. By the Sunday evening, 60 strong and determined women were chosen. This group went to work raising the $600,000 Cdn needed for the project. In the fall of 1996, they held the final selection weekend: pushing limits backpacking over the windy wet moors of Dartmoor, fording rivers, climbing cliffs and abseiling. The selection team was looking for women with stamina, a sense of humor and, most important, team players with initiative and drive. Twenty women were invited to join the Women's Polar Relay.

Nobby (Peter Noble-Jones) also arrived with the first team. He is here to head up the "Keeping the Sponsors Happy" department.

Geoff, Nobby, Denise and I, plus the four women on the first relay, are crammed into a small scuzzy three-bedroom staff house in the village. (Michael and Pen are staying at the "Rookery," up at the airport complex.) To add to our already poor situation, we must share our cramped quarters with two construction workers, who keep the television continuously blasting and pollute the air with cigarette smoke. Every afternoon Denise and I escape for two to three hours to train and continue to test equipment and clothing. I also need the open space to clear my head and the physical work to burn off stress and frustrations.

The fun part of staying in Resolute is meeting the other North Pole expeditions. This year there will be a record number of attempts, seven teams in all.

This evening I went over to see how the Polar Free team are getting on with their final preparations. I had met Nobu, Acchan (from Japan) and Scotty (from New Zealand) back in February when they were in Iqaluit training. We had shared discussions on ski binding problems, worked out how to set up our GPS to "GO TO NORTH POLE" and played with their mini digital camera. They plan to travel unsupported (without any resupplies or assistance from outside) to the Pole, an ambitious undertaking. To haul their 280 kilograms of supplies means that for the first three to five weeks they will pull double loads: hauling a pulk and backpack, then returning to pick up the second load. For every one kilometer of progress, they must travel a total of three kilometers. I am thankful that we only have single loads.

MARCH 3, RESOLUTE, NUNAVUT, CANADA

Time is moving like blowing snow over the land, scraping the rocky ridges bare and depositing deep drifts in the gullies. We are running out of time to work through the glitches and are getting bogged down with so much to do.

Pen and I do not see eye-to-eye on skis. He wants me to use a donated army ski, the same ski he broke on Day Two of his last North Pole attempt. We had agreed on the Fisher E-99 ski and I ordered and shipped 12 pairs to Resolute. I have used Fisher 99s for over 20 years, from teaching ski mountaineering in the Colorado Rockies to numerous expeditions on Baffin Island. The E-99 is also the ski most chosen for Pole trips. Yet Pen still wants to use short 160-centimeter skis because he feels that a shorter ski will be easier for beginners to ski on. I explained that a 160-centimeter ski is constructed to support the weight of a large child. In deep snow or crossing thin ice, it is preferable to have longer skis to distribute your weight.

After a one-hour conversation, Pen asked me to mount one of the army skis, just to try. I was failing to communicate my point. As Paul says, "If your communication doesn't work, change your technique." So I picked up an army ski, walked over to the workbench, stuck the tail of the ski in the vice and pulled back with one hand. SNAP!!! Point made. End of discussion.

On to the Fisher skis, Geoff is mounting the Uni-Flex binding. These bindings are designed to accommodate an insulated winter boot. The binding strap must be altered to incorporate a buckle that can be operated with our thick mittens. I was questioned by the support staff as to whether this was really necessary. They imply that I am too bogged down with my attention to detail. I finally got my point across when I explained that if it takes three minutes every time I take my skis off to climb over a pressure ridge of ice, and another three minutes to put them on, instead of one minute with a modified strap system, then I've wasted five minutes. If we must repeat this exercise an average of ten times a day, in 65 days, we will waste 54 hours. Assuming we travel eight hours a day over a 65-day expedition, we will waste 6.7 days just putting our skis on and taking them off!

As Robert Peary, who claims to have reached the North Pole in 1909, said:

> *The process of reaching the North Pole may be identified with a game of chess, where all the moves, leading to a favorable outcome, have been thoroughly thought out in advance, long before the beginning of the game.*
>
> From the diary of Robert Peary

I am under a lot of stress and our working relationship adds to it. I feel I must constantly and forcefully prove my point with Pen, Michael and Nobby. Any recommendation I suggest is immediately questioned or rejected. They do not acknowledge the years of experience I bring to this expedition. I thought I was getting involved in a "women's" expedition, yet I am constantly confronted by the "old boys' club" approach: "Michael and I have discussed this and we think you should do…." Luckily Geoff understands our situation and provides tremendous support.

This morning, Kohno was flown in to Ward Hunt Island, at the northern tip of Ellesmere. He is the first off to attempt the Pole. Kohno is a Japanese in prime physical condition traveling solo with five resupplies. I wish him success.

I met David Hempleman-Adams at the Co-op store this morning. David, from Great Britain, and his Norwegian partner Rune Gjeldnes, are attempting an unsupported expedition. David has climbed "The Seven Summits," an impressive accomplishment that consists of climbing the highest peak on each of the seven continents. David was the third British climber to complete the seven summits. His driving ambition now is to achieve, in his words, "The Grand Slam." This includes the seven summits plus the four poles: the South Geographical and Magnetic Pole and the North Geographical and Magnetic Pole. Only the North Pole now eludes him. He tried to reach the North Pole in 1983; this will be his second attempt. I wished him luck and he wished me luck, adding, "Don't take it personally if the 'girls' can't do it; I know you can." I replied: "Thanks for believing in me, David, but I think you underestimate these British women." He then went on to say that the last nine British

North Pole expeditions had all failed, including four attempts by the British hero Sir Ranulph Fiennes.

I do wonder what our chances of success are: 30%? 40%? I am optimistic. I'd say we have a 50/50 chance. Around Resolute, after watching the women's attempts to ski, I bet most would think they are generous to give us a 10% chance of making it to the Pole. Time will tell.

It's late at night and time to go to bed.

MARCH 5, RESOLUTE, NUNAVUT, CANADA

The clothing system is a nightmare! Our departure date is eight days away and we are still encountering major problems. The clothing system should have arrived in Iqaluit for me to test by January 15. Only the one-piece suit arrived. Without the entire system, I have not been able to test how it all works together. Parts of the clothing system are still not here. The hood on the one-piece suit is too small to offer face protection and unnecessary, if there is a good hood on the wind jacket. Denise, Geoff and I have spent hours discussing the problems, making numerous phone calls and experiments. Geoff has been a steady pillar of support. But even he is getting stressed about the number of equipment and clothing problems to solve.

The critical problem is the one-piece suit. Never in all my 26 years of leading winter programs have I seen clothing so damp and wet after a day of skiing! The one-piece ski suit takes two days to dry. This worries me. In the Arctic, IF YOU GET WET YOU DIE! (A favorite line of mine.)

It is difficult to determine which layers or materials are causing the water retention. The first layer is a Damart long underwear. I am unfamiliar with this British company and have no idea what the wicking ability is or what they are made of. Cotton? Wool? Polypropylene? Neither the garment label nor the package slip lists the material content. Denise and I will wear our own capeline one-piece long underwear that has provided us with years of comfort. The rest of the team is split: half prefer the polypropylene underwear I had ordered from Helly Hansen; the others are faithful to their donated Damart.

The second layer is the red insulated one-piece suit, designed and sponsored by Vander, a British clothing manufacturer. Denise and I saw the final version of this article when Pen arrived in Resolute. The suits are made of micro fiber—a proven arctic material—but yesterday I learned that treated micro fiber is not breathable... and according to Vander, our generous clothing sponsor, our material "has been carefully treated." Our suits are insulated with Thinsulate, a material more common-ly used in ski and snowmobile apparel, not expedition clothing. Geoff put a piece of Thinsulate in a cup of water and it absorbed water like a sponge.

Today we took action and made drastic modifications. We ripped the Thinsulate out of our glamorous red suits. Pen came by and was shocked to see us ripping apart our new red suits. He inquired, "Matty, what is going on?" I replied, "We are fixing the suits so that they do not retain our perspiration." He was politely told by another women, "If you get wet you die!"

To compensate for the insulation that we are removing, we will add a thick polar fleece Helly Hansen one-piece long underwear. Now we must also add a through-the-crotch zipper to the underwear so it is compatible with the rest of the system. This zipper allows for quick relief of bladder and bowels; exposing the least amount of flesh to the polar elements.

The "smock," an insulated anorak, was to be the third layer. It arrived on March 1 with the 1st team. It's a write-off. Similar to the one-piece suit, it is made of treated micro fiber with Thinsulate insulation. Being insulated makes it too hot to wear while hauling pulks. Yet without it we do not have the wind protection that the hood offers. Today we cut the hoods off the smocks and sewed them to the red one-piece suits.

The final layer was to be a "rest parka" and "rest pant." We still have not seen these and I am unclear what they are. They were to have been insulated, but now it appears that Pen asked for a jacket and pant made of waterproof, breathable fabric. In extremely cold temperatures these Gortex-like materials DO NOT BREATHE!! I am glad that I ordered expedition down parkas from Mountain Equipment Co-op. I have used these parkas with clients for years and they provide excellent warmth. We are scrounging for insulated warm-up pants; Denise has an old pair, I will borrow a pair, two pairs will be sent up from NorthWinds, and we will buy two from the Co-op store here.

For head, hands and feet we are going with a system I have used for many years in the Arctic. For the head a Helly Hansen cowl—a polar fleece head cover with a nylon wind shell. For neck and lower face, we are making polar fleece neck warmers. These can be pulled up to protect the lower part of the face and turned when they ice up from your breath. (These were to have been made in the UK!!!) Double-lens goggles with an added nose guard protect the upper face. For the hands we have— polar fleece wristlets (these we are also making) with polypropylene glove liners, Helly Hansen polar mitts and a pair of expensive expedition mitts. Denise and I are not taking the expedition mitts, as they are made of Gortex and do not breathe. Denise will take her beaver mitts and I my faithful caribou mitts.

On our feet we wear: first a polypropylene sock liner, then a vapor barrier liner (VBL) sock, two pairs of polar fleece socks, and finally the Sorel Expedition boot with double liners good to -100° C. The idea behind the VBL sock is similar to putting a plastic bag over your foot, it prevents the moisture from saturating your insulating layers. Without a VBL sock, after a couple of days of travel, your socks and boot liners would become saturated with moisture and turn into blocks of ice.

This evening, Denise and I were invited to the send-off party for the Dutch team at the High Arctic Lodge. The Dutch team consists of five expedition members: Wilco van Rooijen, Cas van der Gevel, Marc Cornelissen, Edmond Ofner, and Hans van der Meulen, plus a base manager, a camera person and a sound person. They are by far the most organized expedition in Resolute and the most fun and light-hearted. I worked with the Dutch team when they came to Iqaluit to train for a couple of weeks back in December. At dinner we raised our mugs of wine to "Good luck, may the winds blow gently on your back, the leads be frozen, the pressure ridges few…" and other glorious words of encouragement. Before the cake was served, First Air called to say their departure would be delayed because of stormy weather moving in. How frustrating.

MARCH 7, RESOLUTE, NUNAVUT, CANADA

The ski skins are not sticking to the skis in this extreme cold. Ski skins are synthetic fur strips glued to the bottom of cross-country skis to keep the skis from slipping back. I can haul a 40 kilogram pulk without skins but any more and my skis slip backward. Denise is trying to solve this problem. She added Velcro straps over the top of the ski and a bungee strap that wraps around the ski tail. None of these previously proven solutions are working. Today, as a last resort, Geoff will screw the skins to the ski.

The weight of our pulks is steadily increasing. Our pulks are made by Snow Sled, a company specializing in polar equipment and clothing and based in the UK. The puiks are two-meter long fiberglass toboggan/sleds with twin plastic runners on the bottom and a coated nylon cover that zips and buckles closed. A four-meter rope connects the pulk to a shoulder and waist harness worn by the skier. Our pulk weights have now climbed up to 60 kilograms due to a decision to double the number of stoves and the amount of stove fuel. When debating our wet clothing problems, Geoff shared that from his experience in the Antarctic, expeditions have attempted to save weight by carrying the minimal fuel required to cook and melt snow and, therefore, not enough to heat the tent to dry perspiration-damp clothing. Over the weeks that these expeditions traveled, not only did they suffer from the discomfort of damp clothing, but also from the additional burden of hauling the excess weight of the dampness trapped in their clothing and equipment. For example, on Will Steger's 1986 North Pole expedition, he claims their five-kilogram Fiberfill sleeping bags gained up to 20 kilograms of moisture per bag over the course of 65 days! Geoff calculated that if they had taken more fuel, they would have carried less weight in the end! So…the first team will carry an additional 30 liters of fuel plus two more stoves, for a total of 60 liters and four stoves. This, we hope, will provide enough heat in the tent to dry clothing, to ensure a good night's sleep (we sleep in our trail clothes), reduce the chances of frostbite (due to frozen mitts and neck warmers) and provide us with a comfortable morale boost at the end of a long cold day. Some may see comfort as a luxury; I see it, in this instance, as increasing our safety margin.

The Weber tent arrived today. It looks like a giant purple and gold Easter egg. This tent was custom designed for us by Richard Weber and sewed by his wife, Josée. It is an eight-sided tent with a four-meter diameter floor and uses a ski as the center pole. The tent is held up by eight lines anchored in the snow with skis. Ski poles are attached to these lines to prop up the one-meter side walls. To help retain heat, there's a nylon liner inside. To save weight, we will leave the floor behind; I prefer nature's snow-white "carpet." After setting up the tent, Denise and I decided we needed to make a few modifications: inside pockets for personal items, drying lines around the top, and extended snow flaps to pile snow on to keep the walls from blowing in. I am glad I brought my old Singer sewing machine (Bertha) to Resolute: it's been working over time!

The Stephenson sleeping bags also arrived today. These bags were tested by Denise, Paul and me earlier this winter. The five-centimeter foam pad, built into the sleeping system, is a dream to sleep on. However, the vapor barrier liner, sewed into the bag, is not adequate since it allows some perspiration to escape into the down and freeze. This vapor barrier liner uses the same principle as the sock liner used in our boots. Over a number of days this transfer of moisture would cause the down bag to lose loft and insulating value. The solution: add a separate vapor barrier liner made of lightweight coated nylon. When the sleeping bag was tested, we found it barely adequate at -40° C. To compensate for colder temperatures along with exhaustion after a hard day, we added a summer down bag to throw on top and a 50-centimeter Evazote (closed-cell foam) pad under the sleeping bag's built-in foam pad.

MARCH 10, RESOLUTE, NUNAVUT, CANADA

While Denise and I have focused primarily on clothing, equipment, first aid, communication and navigation, Geoff has been training the first team. In the morning, he leads workshops on: polar navigation techniques, prevention, recognition and treatment of cold injuries, winter nutritional needs, stove uses and repair, etc. In the afternoon they are off training, pulling pulks and learning basic cross-country ski techniques. Earlier this week, he took them on a one-night sleep out. This afternoon they returned from a three-day mini-expedition. Geoff is pushing them hard. It is his job to prepare them for the work ahead and to weed out anyone who is not up to the challenge. It is such a relief to know that the women are in good and experienced hands.

The four women who make up the first team are exceptional people. They all have a keen sense of adventure and drive. On the ice, they are fast learners, strong and willing to charge into the unknown. Their enthusiasm to take initiative and experiment with clothing modification and options is reassuring.

Jan McCormac lives in South London. She is a bodyguard for the royal family, with training in crowd control—if anyone looks suspicious, don't ask questions, hit them firmly in the chest and say "Back-up!" This may prove useful if we encounter polar bears. Jan has a good sense of humor, does not take herself too seriously and is the kind of friend one can depend on.

Sue Fullilove, also from London, works as an orthopedic surgeon. Her adventures have taken her cycling 1,931 kilometers across South America and through the Andes. She is a bundle of high frequency energy that never stops. She questions everything Denise and I do and will keep us on our toes.

Claire Fletcher lives in Wexford, Ireland. She is a chiropractor who specializes in working on horses. She has done a number of extended hiking and cycling trips, including 700 kilometers up the coast of Norway. Last year, she sailed across the Atlantic. Claire breeds, trains and races thoroughbred horses. I do not recommend arm-wrestling with this woman.

Ann Daniels is from West Yorkshire. She was the manager at the NatWest Bank in Yeovil when, two years ago, she went through a big career change and became the mother of triplets. Ann has not done any outdoor adventures before. When she decided to try out for the Women's Polar Relay, she went at it with her quiet stubborn determination, often slipping out at night to train when the triplets were asleep.

Denise and I agree that if the next four groups are as strong as this Alpha group, we have no worries about having "the right stuff." The five teams are named: Alpha, Bravo, Charlie, Delta, and Echo, after the phonetic alphabet used on radio calls when transmissions are poor and words need to be spelled out. Rather militaristic. I wonder whose idea.

MARCH 11, RESOLUTE, NUNAVUT, CANADA

There is too much noise in the living room to concentrate on my journal, and its too cold in the room Denise and I share with the sewing machine. There are three centimeters of ice on the inside of the window by my bed. Good acclimatization!

MARCH 12, RESOLUTE, NUNAVUT, CANADA

Two more groups set off today. If the weather cooperates we plan to depart March 14. I can't wait to get out of Resolute and onto the ice. Denise and I had a much-needed night off at the Narwhal Hotel. We spent the morning in the sunny dining room reviewing strategies for ice travel and glueing into our journals communication procedures, codes, maps, magnetic declinations and other charts. For the first time in weeks, we both feel that this expedition is finally coming together. What a relief.

We are the last team to leave Resolute. Ahead of us are:

Kohno	departed on March 3
David Hempleman-Adams	departed on March 4
Pam Flowers	departed on March 4
Polar Free	departed on March 5
Allan Bywater	departed on March 12
Dutch Team	departed on March 12

We heard that Pam Flowers has already called it quits and is returning on the plane that brought the Dutch team north. This was her fourth solo attempt.

MARCH 13, RESOLUTE, NUNAVUT, CANADA

I think…we just might get off the ground. I am getting so excited that I can hardly sit to write!

Today, Denise and I shared our travel strategy with Team Alpha. Here's the plan:

TRAVEL:

Matty and Denise will share the lead. Travel 50 minutes, take a five-minute break. To avoid a traffic jam at pressure ridges, spread out and take different routes. Start with five- to six-hour days and extend as we are physically able to.

PULKS:

Two pulks will carry fuel, 2 will carry food, Denise and I will split the group equipment and also carry food. Denise will carry: radio, PLB (Personal Locator Beacon), Weber tent, two shovels, snow saw and first-aid kit. I will have: Argos (satellite communication backup system), Winchester rifle, repair kit, extra group clothes, four MSR (Mountain Safety Research) stoves, two pots (one for snow melting, one for cooking), billy pot for hot drinks and other cooking items. The four Alpha pulks should weigh 52 kilograms each, while Denise's and my pulks should weigh 45 kilograms, seven kilograms lighter. This allows Denise and me to do more navigation work and—we hope—will keep us from burning out over the long haul.

CAMPING:

From past expeditions, I know that the feeling that not everyone is doing their fair share can slowly erode away the trust between expedition members and destroy an expedition. For this reason, I recommended that we have designated camp duties. After arriving at camp, everyone helps get the tent up. Once done, Sue and Claire shovel snow around the outside snow flap, Ann and I go inside the tent and light the lamp and stoves and begin melting water. Denise and Jan set up the radio. The four outside women hand in equipment and food. As equipment and food are thrown in, Ann and I organize it in its proper place. Inside duties will rotate daily amongst Alpha team members: #1 melt snow, #2 cook dinner, #3 clean up dinner pot, #4 write in group journal. Denise will be responsible for radio calls, I for navigation and keeping the Log Book to date with a.m. and p.m. longitude and latitude, weather including wind speed and direction, temperature, ice conditions, amount of daily drift, team morale, and medical problems.

I can't wait to get out of Resolute, away from phones and faxes, last minute alterations, the pressure of living together in a crowded house, "Has anyone started dinner?" "Where are my socks, I left them right here?" I find myself being pulled in a thousand directions. I am anxious to get out on the ice where we can focus as a team on traveling north!

Ellesmere Island

Day 1 Alpha Day 1

MARCH 14, 1997

5:00 a.m. This is our take-off day! I'm too excited to sleep. I am having coffee and toast, the only food that I can find for breakfast around here, other than Hot Crunchy, which is what I will have to be eating for the next 65 to 75 days. I have a few minutes to write in my journal before giving the wake-up call. If First Air decides the weather is good for flying, we head north at 8:00 a.m. Could I have forgotten anything? I will review my checklists one more time. I am too excited to write.

8:30 a.m. We're in the air! We're off!! According to Russ, our pilot, "visibility is so good that we can see for a day and a half ahead."

I am writing on the plane, crammed into a canvas seat, pulks and parkas piled around me. The noise is deafening in this old Twin Otter and makes conversation, other than mouth-to-ear, impossible. I am sitting up front getting roasted by the heater, while those in the back are freezing.

We landed in Eureka (an Environment Canada weather station) to refuel. We all had to pee so badly that when the doors opened, we leaped out and hurried off to squat behind the nearest oil drum.

The flight over northern Ellesmere Island is spectacular. As we pass over the coast, long fjords cut deep into the mountains and glaciers spill through the rocky peaks. The low sunlight has painted the sea of mountains below in pastel pinks and cold shadowy blues.

I can see Ward Hunt Island! I recognize, from photographs, the dramatic pyramid shape of Walker Hill rising 600 meters high. Ward Hunt Island is surrounded by land-fast ice, extending six kilometers beyond the shore of Ellesmere. This ice does not melt even when the summer returns. I wonder how old this ice shelf is.

Russ Bomberry, a legend among arctic pilots, flew past Ward Hunt Island and out over the sea ice for a preview. He mentioned, in his casual quiet way, that during the last week the ice has become rougher. To me, from 300 meters above, it looks smooth and laced with small wrinkles.

We landed just north of the Parks Canada huts, Quonset structures made of tubular metal frames with plastic canvas covers. The only unlocked hut was a storage work-shop. I hunted around and found the three sled-canoes, left by Will Steger, buried in a snowdrift. Will has generously offered to lend us a canoe if the ice conditions require crossing open water in June. I wanted to look them over and check their con-dition. (Will Steger went to the North Pole with dogs, un-resupplied in 1986. In 1995 he led an expedition that started in Russia and finished at Ward Hunt Island. He used dogs and later changed to these canoe-sleds.)

It was 3:30 p.m. when we finished unloading the Twin Otter. With twilight not far off, I asked the group if they wanted to camp at the hut or to push on. They were split 50/50. Denise and I were also split; Denise wanted to stay, I was for moving on. I wanted to find out just what we were in for. Denise turned to me, "Matty, you decide." I checked the length of the shadows, studied the faces around me and announced, "Let's begin this expedition; let's head to the North Pole!" I walked up the hill to where Pen was testing a radio and told him we were heading out. He was surprised that we were so keen to start even as the sun was setting.

After all the final parting farewells, photos and video shots, we headed north. Out of the shadow of Ward Hunt Island, we skied north, where the sunlight brushed the snow in pink and gold. We traveled over invisible undulations of snow that made the distant ice pack appear and disappear. After two hours, I was really starting to drag; my pulk felt heavier and I began to stagger through the crusty snow. When we stopped to make camp, I saw small bright lights floating all around me. That scared me. I realized, as I fumbled to zip up my down parka with rapidly freezing fingers, that I was hypoglycemic. I was out of energy and fuel. No wonder: with only six hours of restless sleep, three pieces of toast for breakfast, two Penguin bars and a square of chocolate for lunch, my body was in need of FOOD. I felt my core temperature dropping and my hands cooling to the painful stage. I managed to light the stoves and, after a hot drink and a snack, I felt confidently back in control. I'd had a harsh reminder of how unforgiving the Arctic is.

We made Camp #1 at 5:30 p.m. For a long time the sun seemed to rest halfway below the horizon. The wind was breathless and the sky an endless watercolor changing from pink and gold to shades of lavender. I was filled with an overwhelming sense of euphoria.

I feel at home. I am in my element: ice, snow, cold, and limitless horizons. My heart swells to embrace the magic.

Day 2 Alpha Day 2

MARCH 15, 1997

A.M.	latitude N 83° 07.000'	longitude W 74° 14.923'	
P.M.	latitude N 83° 09.629'	longitude W 74° 14.923'	

Distance traveled: 4 nm[1]   *Total nm from Ward Hunt: 4 nm*
Hours traveled: 6 hrs.   *Total nm to North Pole: 412 nm*
Total hours traveled: 8 hrs.   *Temperature: P.M. -36° C*

The sun rose on a clear, cold morning. An hour of skiing brought us to the edge of the ice shelf. From here northward we will travel and camp on the free-floating pack ice. Unlike the Antarctic, where the ice cap is supported by a continent, this northern tip of the planet is covered by a deep, dark polar ocean. Over this ocean, a brittle skin of ice forms, up to approximately 2.5-meters thick in a year[2]. Much of this ice does not melt during the short summer and continues to grow thicker the following winter, becoming multi-year ice up to four-meters thick. Under the ice, strong ocean currents are at work pushing the ice up into "pressure ridges" or cracking it apart to form "leads" of open water. These leads in turn freeze over and become new ice. The prevailing currents over which we will travel are pushing the ice generally southeast. When this south-moving ice collides with the land masses of Ellesmere Island and Greenland it buckles, wrinkles and rises into enormous pressure ridges. These are what we must travel through to reach our elusive goal. These huge pressure ridges are what takes the heart out of many North Pole expeditions.

For hours we skied from pan to pan of multi-year ice, climbing around stone-wall like ridges of ice blocks, the lace-like wrinkles that I saw from the plane. Imperceptibly, the pans grew smaller and the ridges grew larger. As we went on, we were forced to zigzag between ice blocks the size of buildings.

---

1 All distances on the Arctic Ocean are given in nautical miles. One nautical mile equals 1.15 statute mile (regular mile) and 1.85 kilometres.

2 When Peary attempted to reach the North Pole in 1906 and 1909, the new ice was approximately 3.6 metres thick. There is speculation that thinner ice is due to the Greenhouse Effect. Thinner ice means that we faced rougher ice conditions than Peary did since thinner ice breaks up easier and forms pressure ridges.

We are now camped on a small pan of flat ice surrounded by enormous ice blocks. Very scenic but it makes me nervous. We are in a vulnerable position. If the ocean currents begin to push these ice blocks, this pan is too small to offer much protection, and there is not a better place to retreat to.

Inside the tent there is a sense of false security. It is warm with all four MSR (Mountain Safety Research) stoves blasting away. Warm enough, that is, to take off hats and mittens, but not warm enough to take off our trail cloths or melt our floor of snow. While dinner cooks, the jokes are getting silly:

What do you call a man with his legs cut off at the knees? Neil!
What do you call a man with a car on his head? Jack!
What do you call a man standing in a hole? Phil!

I am so glad to be on the trail, moving north, away from all the chaos at Resolute. It's nice to have Paul's old Patagonia pile jacket, the smell of him...a reminder of his support and unshakable faith in me. I use his jacket for a pillow.

Day 3 Alpha Day 3

MARCH 16, 1997

A.M.   latitude N 83° 09.629'   longitude W 74° 14.923'
P.M.   latitude N 83° 10.810'   longitude W 74° 15.562'
Distance traveled: 1 nm   Total nm from Ward Hunt: 5 nm
Hours traveled: 6 hrs.   Total nm to North Pole: 411 nm
Total hours traveled: 14 hrs.   Temperature: P.M. -35° C

There was a taste of gas in the Hot Crunchy cereal this morning. Were the stoves stacked on the food last night? We had to dig out a spare breakfast. (We are carrying five extra days of food in the event that we must continue on in search of a suitable runway or storms delay the changeover to bring in the next relay team.)

Our pulks are heavy. This morning we sorted through the next couple of days of lunches and threw out almost three kilograms of "won't eat" food. The salami is, in the words of Alpha team members, "impossible to eat without gagging," "disgusting," and "putrid." This is serious. The salami accounts for much of our fat requirement. We have not ditched all the salami, hoping that later our need for calories will change our discerning taste buds.

The lunch-snacks hardly resemble the carefully planned menu that Paul worked out on spreadsheets. From hours of research, Paul developed a menu that provided each person between 4,500 and 5,000 calories per day and weighed 900 grams. Over the course of the planning, the assorted nuts were replaced by a donation of peanuts. On paper that was okay, but the peanuts that arrived in Resolute tasted like saltless sawdust. There also should have been a variety of dried fruit; the reality is little cubes of an unrecognizable substance. Assorted candy bars were replaced by a donation of four Penguin bars (chocolate covered biscuits) and four squares of chocolate per day. I had recommend a very good salami, eatable at -40° C. To cut costs, a donation of "a very special" German salami was brought up; as the women said, it's disgusting. By the time I arrived in Resolute, it was too late to make changes and there were rumblings that the expedition could not afford to make replacements. The lack of variety and poor quality of our lunch and snacks concerns me. I fear it may have serious repercussions on our energy levels; which in turn will affect our ability to move safely and keep ourselves from freezing.

Today the ice became too difficult to negotiate with skis on. We set off on foot with our skis strapped on our pulks. Our route crossed table-like pans of ice separated by canals of ice rubble. At the end of each table-like pan, we lowered the pulks down vertical two-meter banks. Then we hauled our pulks along the re-frozen leads, attempting to keep our footing over ice resembling a jumble of enormous ice cubes. To test our sense of humor, our pulks snagged on pinnacles of ice and constantly flipped over. When the canals ended, with teamwork, we lifted the pulks up onto the next small pan. I felt like a rat in a maze, scurrying through narrow cracks, blinded by the high walls of ice, never sure which way offered the route of least resistance.

Pressure ridge after pressure ridge blocked our northward progress. Old refrozen leads offered highways of ice rubble east and west, but nothing opened to the north. After two hours of hauling east then back west, we managed to advance a few hundred meters north of our camp. Depressing! I climbed up an ice pinnacle and could not see an easier route ahead. Denise and I scouted further and came to the conclusion that we were expending too much energy zigzagging. The saying came to mind, "The best way around a problem is straight through it." With two per pulk, we pulled through mountains of towering ice, then returned for the second sled. After endless hours, the ice became relatively smooth and we were able to haul one per pulk again.

In the afternoon we crossed the fresh-looking tracks of the Dutch team. The wind had not blown for three days, so maybe they were not so fresh. We turned off their tracks saying, half in jest, that it might embarrass them if we caught up to them since they started two days ahead of us. As Denise and I searched for "the route of least resistance," we kept finding ourselves back on their tracks.

At 2:45, we came to another zone of heaved-up pressure ice that stretched as far as our limited horizon allowed us to see. The equation for the distance one can see is: d (distance) = the square root of h (height) x 3.6. On the level, at my height of 160 centimeters, I can see four kilometers. From the top of an ice ridge four meters high, plus my height, I should be able to see seven kilometers.

I decided to camp here. We'd pushed continuously for 6 hours with only short stops every hour for a drink, snack and "wee." It was a hard decision. I hated to stop early. We could all have plodded on. But to push on without a pan in sight to camp on seemed unnecessary. My fear was that hauling heavy pulks, as tired as we were, over slippery ice, was to risk an unnecessary injury or to burn out the group.

While I got the stove blasting to melt snow, Denise scouted a route through to the east—ironically, back on the Dutch tracks again.

Day 4 Alpha Day 4

MARCH 17, 1997

A.M. latitude N 83° 10.810'	longitude W 74° 15.562'
P.M. latitude N 83° 14.188'	longitude W 74° 19.332'
Distance traveled: 3 nm	Total nm from Ward Hunt: 8 nm
Hours traveled: 7 hrs.	Total nm to North Pole: 408 nm
Total hours traveled: 21 hrs.	Temperature: P.M. -35° C

Yesterday my pulk was really heavy. Over the last few days, Denise has been taking on weight from other women to lighten their pulks and dumping a good share of it in my pulk. I was working so hard I was dripping sweat. At even short five-minute breaks, I chilled down at an alarming rate. It was more than I could handle to hump that pulk over a hundred bumps. Today, Sue and Claire took some of my weight and I was able to find a pace such that I didn't pour sweat.

Our route today took us over small pans surrounded by pressure ridges. These were aptly described by Jan as "pastures and hedges." We gave up struggling to avoid the Dutch tracks. It was a welcome diversion to read their progress, where they pitched their three tents, where they stopped for a pee, "yup, this one is dehydrated" and left assorted nuts where they stopped for a break. They followed one behind the other...except in the rougher ice where one track went its own way. Denise and I speculated who that might be.

By 3:15 p.m., Sue, now pulling the heaviest pulk, was bushed. Her efforts were heroic. As I experienced yesterday, a pulk even five kilograms too heavy is a burn out. With these heavy loads, we just do not have the power to push longer.

Making camp at 3:00 p.m. in the afternoon and getting to bed by 9:00 p.m. means we are heating the tent for 6 hours at night and another three hours in the morning. We have to be conservative with our fuel consumption. Our ration is four liters per day, which is one liter per stove. Our MSR stoves burn six hours on one liter of fuel.

Attention to detail is a leader's responsibility: therefore the amount of fuel burned, weight of pulks, nautical miles gained per day, what's for dinner—this is what my life is. I was going to say reduced to but it's not reduced in a negative sense; it's just simplified.

Day 5 Alpha Day 5

MARCH 18, 1997

A.M. latitude N 83° 14.188'	longitude W 74° 19.332'
P.M. latitude N 83° 19.000'	longitude W 74° 10.000'

Distance traveled: 5 nm   *Total nm from Ward Hunt: 13 nm*
Hours traveled: 7 hrs.   *Total nm to North Pole: 403 nm*
Total hours traveled: 28 hrs.   *Temperature: P.M. -30° C*

It was very, very cold traveling today: -32° C with a stiff wind from the east. Traveling at -32° C on a windless day is not unpleasant—that is, if you are dressed appropriately, are well rested, and have a full tank of calories. It is the wind chill that makes life miserable. It sucks the life heat away from my body and blows my frosted ruff around my hood into my face, decreasing my visual world.

We traveled over opaque leads covered in "chrysanthemum crystals." This is the name I've given to these delicate crystals that grow like the rays of a flower with three- to six-centimeter long spikes. As I plod along I wonder what causes crystals to grow in different forms. My guess is that it has to do with the way salt water freezes and sublimates from the relative warmth of a newly frozen lead into the extreme cold of the air at the top of the planet. Perhaps the different crystal formations are caused by variations in temperature and amount of salt in their make-up.

The afternoon found us on a series of endless small pans with about one to two meters of ice rubble between the pans. Over and over we hauled the pulks up and over. And over and over the pulks flipped or caught on ice chunks. (If you're thinking that reading over and over is monotonous, just imagine how we felt.) The small of my back hurts from the thousand times my pulk came to an abrupt halt. Most of today I hauled without the waist belt, just the shoulder straps, to give the small of my back a break.

Navigating is interesting—that is, different and challenging. Normally, in my other life back on Baffin Island, I rely on my map-reading skills to translate the contour lines on the map to the contours of the hills and valleys around me. Up here the earth is flat and a map useless for determining location. Using a compass is dicey at this latitude. We are 800 kilometers from the Magnetic North Pole. At our present location our magnetic declination is 86° west. This means that the north on our compass is in the correct position when the compass needle points 86° to the west (counter clockwise from north). At this distance from the Magnetic North Pole the compass needle is sluggish in settling towards magnetic north. It is fascinating and disconcerting to see the compass needle swing 90°! Just when I think the needle has stopped, it swings 45° the other way. I get impatient waiting for the needle to settle. As we move further from the Magnetic Pole, our compass will perform better.

Back in the early days of polar exploration, it was necessary to use a sextant to measure the angle of the sun above the horizon. The angle, the date and exact time had to be looked up in a log book to find the explorer's latitude and longitude. To navigate by sextant one needs skill, knowledge, and the ability to see the sun[3]. In the new age of satellites we now have Global Positioning Systems, called GPSs. A GPS triangulates your location from a number of satellites. We do not use our GPS during

---

3 Later in May we did not see the sun for days because of overcast weather.

the day when we are traveling because they rely on batteries and batteries have a short life in extremely cold temperatures. Every night, after the stoves are fired up, Denise and I hang our GPSs at the top of the tent to thaw them. After an hour we turn them on to get our latitude and longitude. The GPS is also able to give us the distance to the North Pole, the magnetic declination (degrees off true north that we must adjust our compass), and the distance from any of our last campsites.

During the first few days of the expedition, Denise and I were able to shoot a compass bearing from one prominent ice form to the next. In this way, it was not necessary to ski on a straight course to get to our next prominent ice marker. We would find the route of least resistance. Once arrived at our ice marker, we would shoot our next bearing. This is now an impossibility: traveling through this war zone of ice rubble, there is no prominent ice form that stands out, so I judge our east-west swing with a visual back bearing off Walker Mountain against the high mountain behind it. If Walker Mountain is to the right of the mountain, we are swinging too far east, if it is to the left, we are too far west.

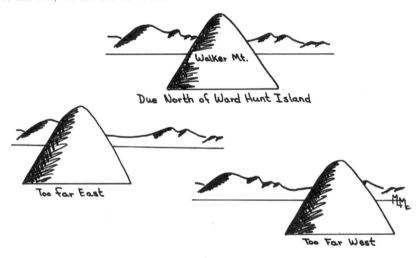

The navigational tool that I rely on the most is the sun's shadow and my watch. At noon "local time," the sun is due south. To figure out our local time, I must know which meridian (north-south lines of longitude) we are traveling on and Greenwich Mean Time (GMT). The GPS tells me we are traveling on the 74th meridian. Before leaving Resolute, I set the watch on my left wrist to GMT. To work out my local time, I must divide our meridian by 15. The 15 comes from the fact that the sun moves 15 degrees every hour. So 74 divided by 15 equals roughly five therefore, our local time is roughly five hours behind GMT. When it is 17:00 hours or 5:00 p.m. in Greenwich, it is 12:00 noon where I stand. I adjust the watch on my right wrist five hours behind GMT to give me our local time. It is important to know exactly what our local time is because, as I said earlier, at local noon, the sun is exactly due south and casts a shadow due north, directly towards the North Pole. Knowing that the sun moves 15 degrees every hour, I use the following method to navigate:

at 09:00 a.m., my shadow is 45° west (left) of true north
at 10:00 a.m., my shadow is 30° west (left) of true north
at 11:00 a.m., my shadow is 15° west (left) of true north
at 12:00 noon, my shadow points to true north
at 01:00 p.m., my shadow is 15° east (right) of true north
at 02:00 p.m., my shadow is 30° east (right) of true north
at 03:00 p.m., my shadow is 45° east (right) of true north

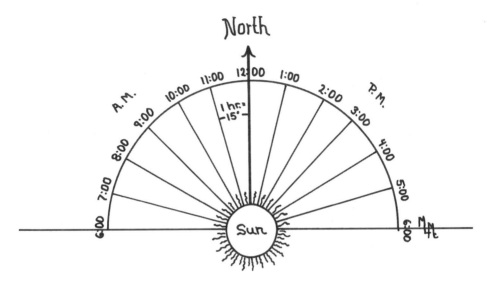

From all the accounts that I had read of past expeditions, I was expecting it to be colder and darker. I knew that the sun first touched northern Ellesmere on March 4. I estimated it would be dark at night for the first leg of the relay. Wrong! We used the Coleman lamp only for the first few nights. It was dusk inside the tent and hard to see if the pot was about to boil over or to write in our journals. Now, even when I get up for a quick 3:00 a.m. pee, it's light.

Day 6 Alpha Day 6

MARCH 19, 1997

A.M.   latitude N 83° 19.000'   longitude W 74° 10.000'
P.M.   latitude N 83° 24.613'   longitude W 74° 15.184'
Distance traveled: 6 nm   Total nm from Ward Hunt: 19 nm
Hours traveled: 7 hrs.   Total nm to North Pole: 397 nm
Total hours traveled: 35 hrs.   Temperature: P.M. -30° C

Today is Sue's birthday! She's 31. She has invited us all to her party.

We turned off the Dutch track and headed due north, shooting bearings from ice tower to ice tower. Our route north crossed the predominant east-west snowdrifts. My day consisted of: kicking toe holds into snow dunes to get to the top of the drift, dragging my pulk up hand-over-hand and fast footing it down the other side so the pulk didn't run me over when it came careening down. Often, as I was running forward to get out of the pulk's descent, it would catch on a small drift and come to an abrupt halt, slamming me into my harness. Over, and over, and over, all day long.

If you like forced marches, you would enjoy our daily travel routine. "Forward march," tromp, tromp, for 50 minutes. "Break time," five to ten minutes to pee, gulp down 1/4 of my water bottle, eat a chunk of salami, Penguin bars, chocolate squares, granola bars. "Last call" (one minute before we head out), "Prepare to mount up" (put harness on) and "Go to North Pole" (head out). "One little step for Penguins, one giant step for womankind" (our little joke). Work like a dog for 20 minutes before hands are re-warmed, then another 20 minutes before I need to unzip underarm and leg vents. About the time that I am comfortably warm, it's time for another break.

At our 3:00 p.m. break, we came to a large expanse of ice rubble. While the group took a rest, Denise and I scrambled up a ridge to scout. I summed up our observation to the group, "The bad news is that it looks like hell to the north. The good news is that we saw a lake-size lead 1/4 of a nautical mile to the west. This lead appears to go north-northeast. I recommend that we detour over to the lead to gain some smooth gliding." Sue must not have grasped the concept that we were going west to eventually gain easier miles north. Shortly after I set off she hollered, "Matty, you must go north! Why are you going west?" After we reached the lead and were making excellent mileage north, Sue's faith in my leadership was restored. She kept saying, "Matty, that was brilliant!"

I didn't feel brilliant, just damned lucky that the edge of this open lake-like lead was frozen enough to allow us to glide along past all that endless ice rubble. The lip of ice was an opaque white and not very thick, so I asked everyone to put skis on and lengthened pulk traces in order to better distribute our weight. The color of the ice is an indication of its thickness: black ice is just a thin skin of transparent ice floating on the black sea, opaque ice is thin and rubbery, white ice is thicker. As we skied, the open water five meters to our left rippled from the vibrations of our movements.

It was great to have skis on again and to be making miles.

At 4:00 p.m. we made camp on a flat section of shoreline where the lead turned northeast. I wonder if this is what Robert Peary called The Big Lead, where he was held up for a week waiting for it to freeze. Richard Weber said that he himself never encountered a big lead, but instead, a river of moving ice pans. After all our hard work to pull through the hell of pressure ice now behind us, will we be halted by The Big Lead?

After dinner I went out for an evening promenade and watched the sun ever so slowly sink into the mist rising from the open water. The mist, back-lit by the setting sun, was an intense gold. An arctic version of a peaceful summer evening at the cottage On Golden Pond. I wonder what Paul, Eric and Sarah are doing tonight.

Day 7 Alpha Day 7

MARCH 20, 1997

A.M.   latitude N 83° 24.613'   longitude W 74° 15.184'
P.M.   latitude N 83° 30.432'   longitude W 74° 09.912'
Distance traveled: 5 nm   Total nm from Ward Hunt: 24 nm
Hours traveled: 7 hrs.   Total nm to North Pole: 392 nm
Total hours traveled: 42 hrs.   Temperature: P.M. -23° C

This morning, Denise and I surveyed The Big Lead from the top of an ice ridge. The lead seemed to curve to the northeast beyond our range of vision. I couldn't believe our luck! The band of open water that had rippled yesterday as we skied was frozen! Well, sort of frozen. Denise and I skied out with a throw-line rescue bag and the ice ax to test the thickness of the ice. The new ice varied between opaque and black ice, a bit rubbery and a thin three-centimeters thick. The ice beyond the new ice was a more reassuring ten centimeters. Ten centimeters is good. I would not like to cross a two kilometer span of new ice; a rescue would be impossible in such a situation. Too risky! If someone went through the thin ice here, close to shore, it would be possible to throw the rescue rope from the safety of the thicker old ice that we camped on.

I decided to cross the lead where it was only two kilometers wide and head north along the far shoreline. Extending across from our camp was a line of new ice "rafted" (one layer of ice sliding over another), creating a thicker layer. This was our projected line of travel. Anticipation ran high as water bottles were filled, stoves shut down, tent dropped, pulks packed and skis strapped on.

Jan did not sleep well last night. She had disturbing dreams of falling through the ice and being pulled down into the dark sea by her pulk. To avoid her fear of open water, she had requested to be on the first relay team, where there would be more pressure ice and fewer open leads. Today she had to face her worst nightmare. Jan asked to ski behind me.

I led across the dark band of thin ice. When I was across, Jan followed, then Ann, Sue and Claire, with Denise bringing up the end with the throw-line rescue bag.

The sun was warming our confidence. There was not a breath of wind. The earth was silent under a frozen blanket of snow and ice; the only sounds were the swish, swish of our skis and the chick, chick of our ski poles. For a long time the far shoreline refused to get closer. Jan skied with her head down, not daring to look up. Every so often, in a shaking voice, she'd ask, "Matty, how far are we?" I'd respond in my most reassuring voice, "Almost half way," "More than half way now," "Almost there."

To add to Jan's trepidation, a mysterious rumbling sound started to the north. The noise coming across the ice sounded like freight trains crashing together. It was uncanny how it seemed only a few hundred meters away. In the Arctic's clear dry air, sounds travel more easily.

On the far shore we took a break and congratulated ourselves on our successful crossing of The Big Lead. I was thankful for our luck and thrilled to see miles of easy travel northward on the edge of The Big Lead. The temperature being a warm -23° C, we took a longer relaxing break than planned before pushing onward towards the unexplained thunder. It was exciting; my adrenaline was flowing. The winds were calm, the ice motionless. Somewhere the ocean currents were shoving large blocks of ice. It was not until we were passing the area of rumbling and stopped to listen that we saw large blocks of ice rubble tumble onto the thin ice covering the lead and breaking through. We were traveling on this thin ice! As captivating as this show was to watch, we chose to move away, quickly.

Further up The Big Lead we saw more signs of ice movement. Mesmerized, we stopped to watch one slab of ice raft up over another. The sounds were amazing, "Squeak, squeak, squeak..." as the ice moved in rhythmic jerks. Even Jan unglued her eyes from her skis and was thrilled by the sight. I pulled out my camera and took a photo of the ice advancing on my ski tracks and, a minute later, a photo with the ice pushing over my tracks!

By afternoon the ice on The Big Lead became progressively more fractured. At one point, Denise led across a small crack. By the time the last one of us arrived, the lead had opened two meters! We skied along on opposite sides of the newly opened lead, joking back and forth. "Well at least we have the tent." "So, we have the stoves, pots and dinner!" Not the kind of thing to joke about. Before the jokes wore thin we found a narrow place to cross. While crossing, Ann's pulk took a shortcut and slid into the water. There was lots of shouting, "Ann, your pulk's in the water; hurry, hurry, pull it out!" I was more concerned for Ann and called out, "Take your time Ann; get yourself across first. Your pulk is fine, it's floating." After she was safely across I added: "And thanks for testing the floatability of our pulks." I had been fairly confident that our pulks would float, but just how high in the water I didn't know. It was reassuring to see that Ann's pulk floated high enough to keep her gear dry.

I enjoy skiing on newly frozen leads. They offer new challenges and it's a pleasant break from the monotony of snow dunes and pressure ridges. The best part, though, is that we can make easy miles.

Near the end of the afternoon, it became increasingly more difficult to find a route through the maze of cracked ice. The Big Lead started to veer to the east. Time to leave it and head north into another nightmare of pressure ridges, snow hummocks and refrozen leads. It was with reluctance that I turned away from The Big Lead, a shimmering silver sea merging with the horizon into mystical light that extended into limitless space. A mirage of ice castles floating above the silver sea added to the surreal image. I did not bother to take a parting photo—I don't possess the photographic skills to capture the expanse and depth of that magical arctic light. It will remain the most marvelous picture in my mind.

We made camp under the broad heavens, a minuscule dot on the immense expanse of polar ice. I enjoy the sensation of feeling so small and insignificant. It shrinks all my worries to specks of dust. Our GPS indicated a gain of five nautical miles north. I had expected better mileage traveling on The Big Lead. Tonight is radio night. We have "sched calls" (scheduled radio calls) with our base in Resolute every other night.

After the pre-arranged exchange of information on: location, weather, ice and next-scheduled radio call, Michael, in a very serious voice, asked us to hold. We waited in suspense wondering what bad news he had for us. Had a family member died? Was the expedition out of money and over for us? Michael returned to the radio. "There is an enormous lead ahead of you. It held up the Dutch team for two days. According to the satellite photos, it stretches to Greenland!" We couldn't wait for him to stop talking so Denise could answer: "Not a problem. We crossed it today!" There was a long pause before Michael responded in a surprised and relieved voice, "Splendid! Well done!"

We also learned that we are now ahead of Alan Bywater and David Hempleman-Adams and his Norwegian partner. This is not much to gloat about since both are going without resupply and hauling double loads. I expect that they will catch up to us when they are down to a single load. We also learned that Kohno, the solo Japanese, has passed 84°, and that both the Dutch and Polar Free (Scotty, Nobu and Acchan) are only a few miles ahead of us. That's good news. Since the Dutch have resupplies, it means that our excruciatingly slow rate of travel is still respectable in relation to the other physically stronger male groups.

Day 8 Alpha Day 8

MARCH 21, 1997

A.M.	latitude N 83° 30.432'	longitude W 74° 09.912'
P.M.	latitude N 83° 35.789'	longitude W 74° 11.436'
Distance traveled: 5 nm		Total nm from Ward Hunt: 29 nm
Hours traveled: 7 hrs.		Total nm to North Pole: 387 nm
Total hours traveled: 49 hrs.		Temperature: P.M. -30° C

Day eight and only 66 more days to the Pole—that is, if we make it for Denise's birthday on May 26 as I planned.

Today, I struggled with my melancholy mood. It's hard to make this trudging and hauling fun. My knees are burning out from pulling, the small of my back is on fire and screams when the pulk slams to an abrupt halt, and my face hurts from the frost-coated fur around it. Of late, my thoughts have gotten stuck, like a broken record, on a jumble of words. Sometimes I'm stuck on a monotonous patter: "right ski, left ski, right ski, left ski" or "Go to North Pole, Go to North Pole." Other times it's part of a tune, "It's been a hard day's night and I've been working like a dog" or "Staying alive, staying alive..." At first it's kind of like a mantra, soothing and hypnotic. A great mind-body escape—until I want to think of other important matters and find that my thoughts continue to get interrupted with "right ski, left ski, right ski, left ski..." Getting unstuck is becoming an effort.

As I skied, I reflected on the contrast between the infinite personal space that I have, from horizon to horizon during the day, compared to the limited one square meter of personal space that I am confined to in the tent. In some way one offsets the other; the overpowering vastness is the opposing balance to the cramped confines of the tent.

Day 9 Alpha Day 9

MARCH 22, 1997

A.M. *latitude N 83° 35.789'*	*longitude W 74° 11.436'*
P.M. *latitude N 83° 41.667'*	*longitude W 74° 13.713'*
Distance traveled: 7 nm	*Total nm from Ward Hunt: 36 nm*
Hours traveled: 7 hrs.	*Total nm to North Pole: 380 nm*
Total hours traveled: 56 hrs.	*Temperature: P.M. -35° C*

It was an interesting day. It did seem colder, -35° C with a light northwest wind. All our breaks were short. The silent cold stole into our sweat-drenched clothing, a sharp reminder to keep moving. It took a full 30 minutes of hard hauling to rewarm my hands—very scary when it takes that much time and blood-pumping work to re-warm.

A bird flew over our heads today. How odd. We are so far from land. It looked like a short-neck duck, but it is only March 22, too early for ducks, who only reach south Baffin in May. It was silhouetted against the sky so that I couldn't see its color. Could it have been a high-flying ptarmigan, lost or out for a cruise? (Ptarmigans are one of the few birds to winter over in the Arctic. Their splotchy brown summer camouflage turns to white in the winter. They look like small chickens walking around on large feathered feet and fly only short distances when they have to.)

By 3:00 in the afternoon, the wall of low clouds that had been sneaking in from the south overtook us. The lighting became flat, ice and sky merged into the same shadowless gray. If it wasn't for gravity, I would have no way of knowing earth from sky. By the time we set up camp, visibility had decreased to less than 100 meters.

I wonder how things are at home. Is Sarah practicing the cello? Eric should have flown south today to accompany his grandmother home to Smooth Rock Falls after her operation in Ottawa. How is Paul coping with my absence? Is his life more or less stressful now that I am on the trail?

We accomplished a record seven nautical miles north! We have pushed for nine days without a day off. From studying past accounts of previous expeditions, I expected a storm/layover day about once a week. So far every day has been cold and clear. I can't risk taking a layover day when the weather is good. No telling what tomorrow will bring.

We are 36 nautical miles north of Ward Hunt Island and have now achieved our projected mileage for this relay team. Alpha Team was scheduled to be on the ice for 15 days. I estimated a half-day for changeover at the start, two storm/layover days, plus a half-day for changeover at the end, for a total of 12 travel days. Knowing that the ice at the start would make for some difficult traveling, I planned a conservative three nautical miles a day. For the sake of keeping up morale, it is far better to be conservative. Twelve travel days x 3 nm a day = 36 nm. It's a good feeling to be ahead, to have miles in the bank against any future bad luck.

Tonight's news from our sched call is that Paul called Resolute to pass on his love and support. That's nice. We are now well ahead of David Hempleman-Adams and Alan Bywater. Alan seems to be having difficulties but Michael could not, or would not, elaborate. We asked about the position of the Polar Free and Dutch teams but Michael refused to give us this information. I can respect that he likes to be professional and not gossip on the radio, BUT we feel that he is patronizing and editing which information we need and withholding information that HE feels will distract us.

The reason we like to know where the other teams are is simply to use their progress as a measuring stick. On this trackless expanse of ice there are no signposts to indicate whether we are doing a respectable job or making fools of ourselves.

As I trudge along during the day, I play with thoughts that I wish to capture in my journal. But by evening, I have forgotten them or they have lost their profound significance. Here is today's tidbit of information: Denise and I give names to ice formations that mark our bearing (direction). In all this ice rubble, it helps us remember which, out of the multitude of ice chunks, we are heading towards. Today we named our ice markers: the big marshmallow, frog, rabbit on the hill, wagon wheel, purple mountain, polar bear head and snaggle tooth. As soon as it's on paper it looks silly. Have my thoughts regressed to this level of simplicity?

With four stoves blasting around the center tent pole, it's a sauna in here. Having the ability to warm this tent is our security blanket, providing a much-needed break from the stress of a long cold day on the trail. It's so warm that we all stripped down for a sponge bath. A great morale booster. After our sponge bath we shut off two stoves. In a couple of hours, the damp mittens, neck warmers and glove liners hanging at the top of the tent will be dry. Sleeping in dry clothing means a tolerable night's sleep.

Day 10 Alpha Day 10

MARCH 23, 1997

A.M.   latitude N 83° 41.667'   longitude W 73° 03.586'
P.M.   latitude N 83° 41.711'   longitude W 73° 50.626'
Distance traveled: 0 nm   Total nm from Ward Hunt: 36 nm
Hours traveled: 0 hrs.   Total nm to North Pole: 380 nm
Total hours traveled: 56 hrs.   Temperature: P.M. -20° C

Just when I was wondering if the weather would ever force us to take a day off, it has hammered in on us. I am always the first up, and this morning, hearing the wind battering the tent, I decided to check the weather before giving the "Rise and Shine" call. Getting out of the tent tunnel door was the first problem. Northerly winds had deposited a snowdrift across the door. I grabbed a stove board to shovel my way out. The weather was definitely nasty. After a most disagreeable pee, with spindrift snow blowing in every fold of clothing, I checked the thermometer. It was only -20° C. The Wind Wizard measured the wind speed at 40–60 kph. My compass confirmed a north wind. Once inside, the weather report I gave was, "Blowing like hell, visibility two meters, so enjoy your sleep-in. If it lets up this morning, we'll push on after lunch." To push on in this weather is a waste of energy. Anyway, we needed a rest day.

After the luxury of a sleep-in, we rolled up our sleeping systems and fired up the stoves. Denise did her morning ritual of making us both a mug of coffee. She starts with one tablespoon of non-instant powdered milk, adds a little water, stirs it like an electric mixer to avoid lumps, adds one coffee bag, two lumps of sugar and fills our mugs with boiling water. Breakfast is the usual Hot Crunchy cereal, with more lumpy powdered milk. The powdered milk is packed in the cereal, for trail simplicity and to save on packaging. I hate getting the last serving at the bottom of the bag where most of the powdered milk ends up. When I add water to the cereal it turns to lumpy white mud. Yuck! As they say in Britain, "Mustn't grumble."

After breakfast, I take some time to write in my journal. As I am writing, Denise sews her mega-wolf ruff back to keep it out of her eyes. Sue is studying medical reports. (The crazy things that people bring on expeditions would make an interesting book!) Ann has cut her book into chapters to share with Jan. Claire is reading.

It's been a fun day. We've had lots of laughs. Jan, with solicited input, wrote up a list of Top Tips on Toileting in the group journal.

1. Select a proper site: out of the wind, with a good selection of firm snow wedgies handy and check that surface is absorbent (weeing on ice splatters).

2. Quickly remove mitts, reach between legs, locate zipper, pull and unzip, reach back for long underwear zipper, carefully unzip to avoid catching pubic hairs; as you squat, grab material and pull aside.

3. Let her rip, check your aim and reposition if necessary.

4. Select appropriate snow wedgie (large enough to keep gloves clean, remove sharp edges, avoid using fluffy stick-on-your-bum snow).

5. Zip up quickly but with care.

At the time it seemed ridiculously funny.

Tonight on the radio we asked for a weather update. Michael called back. First Air told him that this stormy weather may continue for another day. We asked for news of other groups. Michael would not say. It seems the Resolute support team is intentionally withholding information from us again. After the sched call, heated conversations raged between the relay women on why they were doing this to us. "Do they think we are not mature enough to deal with the truth?" "Do they think that we are trying to catch up to the Dutch because we said that they were cute?" It sure as hell does not elicit our trust in our base team. This withholding of information is causing a "We/They" division within the expedition. Not good. If the situation becomes serious out here on the ice, what kind of support can we count on?

We turned on the radio at 6:30 p.m. to catch the Dutch sched call. We learned that Alan Bywater "had fallen into a lead and lost his pulk," stumbled into David Hempleman-Adams' camp and was rescued by David and Rune. They nursed him until a plane was able to evacuate him. When the Dutch finished with "listening out," (listening out means that both parties leave the radio on for another minute in case anyone remembers something else that needs to be communicated) we cut in. "Dutch Expedition, Dutch Expedition, this is Alpha Polar Relay." Marc came on, "This is Dutch Expedition, you are coming in clear, Alpha Polar Relay." (They are only 12 nm north of us.) Marc enthusiastically congratulated us on how well we were doing, "You are doing great, you are doing great!" Those words, coming from a fellow ice-traveler, one who knows what we face, filled us with such happiness and a warm glow of pride. It made Michael's, "Well done, girls," ring hollow in comparison.

At 7:00 p.m. we caught David's radio call. He kept asking his Resolute man, "Did you get Alan on film when he got off the plane in Resolute? Did we look good with the rescue? Did we look good? Did we look good?" What an ego! He continued on about his BBC and CBC coverage. He also alluded to a big publication deal pending, but said that, because others might be listening in, he wouldn't mention the publisher. That gave us a good laugh! He didn't give his position, but we know that we are miles ahead of him. He never gives his position on the radio! Our competitive nature is enjoying being ahead of him, but to be fair David and Rune are attempting an unsupported expedition and are hauling pulks at least three times the weight of ours.

Day 11 Alpha Day 11

MARCH 24, 1997

A.M.	latitude N 83° 41.667'	longitude W 74° 03.586'
P.M.	latitude N 83° 44.860'	longitude W 73° 43.340'
Distance traveled: 3 nm	Total nm from Ward Hunt: 39 nm
Hours traveled: 5 hrs.	Total nm to North Pole: 377 nm
Total hours traveled: 61 hrs.	Temperature: P.M. -29° C

A.M. (written in morning): We are still stormbound. Yesterday it was a treat to have a layover day. Today we are itching to get out of the confines of this tent and make some miles north! According to the GPS, we drifted to the east last night, over the 74th meridian. That is not good. If we drift too far east, we will get caught in the Trans Polar Drift that will carry us towards Greenland.

P.M. (written in evening): We were so anxious to get going that by noon we imagined that the weather was clearing. Sometimes it is better for group morale to move than to go stir-crazy sitting in the tent. We packed up, stuffed the wildly flapping tent into its stuff sac and headed off into a world of swirling snow. Before the back of the line had started, I fell onto an invisible three-meter snow dune and had to feel my way around it, circling almost back to our campsite. To add to the frustration of poor visibility and flat lighting, my goggles kept fogging up. The spindrift of fine snow found its way into even the smallest cracks: zippers, pockets, mitten cuffs, goggles, around head cowl, neck warmer and fur ruff. Not a particularly pleasant experience.

At about 1:30 p.m. I unknowingly stepped over a 15-centimeter crack. Claire followed, then Sue. I heard Ann yell. Something in her tone sounded like trouble. When I looked back, Sue was scrambling out of a waist-deep crack. Luckily, only her right foot got wet. In less than a minute her boot was encased in solid ice: "Slushy on the inside, crusty on the outside." We were in a windy area and so headed to the lee of the nearest ice block. While I dug out a spare pair of boot liners from my pulk, Ann located dry socks and warmed them in her parka. To release the frozen cordlocks on the boot laces, it was necessary to pour hot water (from a water bottle) over them.

Later in the afternoon, our northerly direction was halted by a six- to ten- meter wide open lead running northwest. We detoured along the lead for a kilometer without finding a narrows or bridge to cross. When the lead turned west, we stopped and made camp. We hope this lead will freeze over or close during the night.

I was thinking of the story that Fritz (Dr. Koerner) told me about taking all day to cross a lead on the trans-polar expedition with Wally Herbert. "It took us all day to cross the lead. We engineered a boat by lashing two dog sleds together and wrapping them in tarps. The dogs had to swim across while we used skis to paddle our sled-raft over. At the end of the day we were so exhausted that we made camp beside the open lead. That night the lead closed." If we are patient, we may be lucky.

The GPS still indicates that we are at 73° 43,' even though I led northwest all day. Tomorrow we will try again to get back to 74°.

Tonight, Ann, under Denise's coaching, did the radio call. Michael dropped an emotional bomb when he suggested that our changeover, scheduled for the 28th, be moved to the 30th in order to split the charter with the Dutch team. Ann was at a loss and did not know how to reply so asked Michael to hold. Emotions were high. We had a quick discussion. Yes, it was logical to save thousands of dollars by splitting the charter cost. But, emotionally the Alpha women were only mentally and physically prepared to push on for another three days. The two additional days made it seem like a week. Sue was concerned about getting back to work late and Ann was anxious to see her babies. After the initial shock passed the group finally came to a consensus: "Yes," Ann responded to Michael, "if it is best for the expedition it is okay with us."

We also talked to Bravo Team on the radio. They are camped on the ice outside Resolute, training with Geoff. They sounded enthusiastic and in awe of the Arctic. Michael came back on the radio. His parting remark, before listening out, was that he had heard us talking to the Dutch team the other night. That did not deter us from tuning in to catch the Dutch tonight! After Marc gave their latitude and longitude, he switched to speaking Dutch. Darn! Denise quickly calculated that they are now 14 nautical miles ahead and have drifted quite a ways to the east of us.

After the flood of negative emotions around extending their time on the ice, the women are already swinging around to embrace the challenge. They are amazing! They are now fired up about making their original goal of reaching the 84th latitude.

Day 12 Alpha Day 12

MARCH 25, 1997

A.M.   latitude N 83° 45.388'   longitude W 73° 38.273'
P.M.   latitude N 83° 50.313'   longitude W 73° 46.514'
Distance traveled: 5 nm   Total nm from Ward Hunt: 44 nm
Hours traveled: 6 hrs.   Total nm to North Pole: 372 nm
Total hours traveled: 66 hrs.   Temperature: P.M. -33° C

A.M. When I went out for my last pee during the night, I noticed that the lead had widened to 50 meters. This morning I can hear some action out there. The lead has closed to the east and, where the two pans of ice come together, the ice is pushing enormous blocks of ice. Already a nine- meter pressure ridge has developed and continues to grow as we gulp down our breakfast. This is exciting. From the tent we can see monster ice blocks tumbling off the rising mountain and splashing into the water.

P.M. After scouting to the east and west, we realized that the only place to cross was where the open water and pressure ridge met. We unclipped from our pulks and watched for an appropriate moment to cross, such as when the ice blocks stopped moving. Our planned route was to take us along the lower edge of this unstable ridge. While preparing to cross, Ann stepped into the soft snow at the side of the lead and got her foot, or rather the outside of her boot, wet. With adrenaline flowing, one at a time we scrambled along the edge and jerked our pulks along. I loved the excitement. I would not call myself an adrenaline junky, but this sure breaks the monotony.

For the next hour we crossed and, to our frustration, recrossed a number of small open leads. On smaller cracks we managed to jump over; others we crossed on "floaters." "Floaters" is my term for the large ice chunks that float in the open leads. Some are large enough to support our weight, while smaller ones slowly sink or tip when you put your full weight on them.

After the maze of cracks it was back to hauling over snow dunes again. To add to today's challenges, soft powder snow from the storm had accumulated in between the dunes. It was such exhausting work to break trail that Denise and I exchanged leading after every break. To pull my pulk through the deep snow, I had to lean at such an angle that my boots slipped out from under me and I dropped on all fours. I now have matching bruised shins.

At 3:00 p.m. we saw a dark ominous mist due north of us. Our suspicions were confirmed by a large lake-like lead, so wide that the far shore was obscured by the gloomy mist. We turned west and slogged along the shore, hoping this was the shortest route around the lead. At what appeared to be the end, were hills of moving ice rubble grinding and toppling into the lead. We stood in the freezing wind to listen and watch house-size chunks of ice tumble in the water, sink, then bob up and flop over like beached whales.

The thought of being forced to camp in the moving rubble did not appeal to me, so we made camp on a large flat pan well back from the shifting ice. As I write I can hear the freight-train-like sounds of screeching brakes, crashing cars and slow rumblings. Denise went for an evening walkabout and nearly didn't make it back to camp. While she was taking a picture, the trickster-ice began to open up behind her. When she realized what was happening, she took a flying leap across the opening crack and made a lucky landing on the other side.

I worry how I will solve getting around this moving ice tomorrow. I can feel the weight of the responsibility tonight. I hope the noise of the crushing ice will not keep me awake.

We turned on the radio to catch David Hempleman-Adams. They are at 83° 14' but have a one-meter hole in one of their pulks. The Polar Free are still relaying loads through the pressure ice but are now able to pull both loads on smooth refrozen leads. Coms (communications) were not clear; we think they said they are at 83° 44' and have drifted to W 72°.

It was such hard going today that my lower back is screaming, knees hurt, and legs ache from the strain. It was a cold -33° C with a 30 kph wind. The wind kept pushing my frosted black bear ruff into my face, causing a sharp sting that demanded I do something or my face would freeze. At -40° C, with a 10-kph wind, exposed skin freezes in less than 30 seconds.

How can I do this for another 65 days?!! Am I just overly tired today? Maybe I am too old (I am 45). Or is my heart really not into this? I would throw more heart and soul into this expedition if I had been more involved from the beginning with the selection of the women, with more time to test equipment and clothing, and more time to mentally prepare. It has been hard to let go of family and my NorthWinds business for four months. It's not as if I can take a weekend off, or call and talk to them. It is so discouraging to compare the 44 nautical miles we have covered from Ward Hunt to the 372 miles we still have to travel to reach the North Pole.

I know I'm whining. All day I have to be a brave fearless leader. My journal is the only outlet I have to air my negative feelings before throwing them to the winds. Jan had a low day too. She fell into six holes! So what do I have to complain about?

9:00 p.m., bedtime.

Day 13 Alpha Day 13

MARCH 26, 1997

A.M.   latitude N 83° 50.296'   longitude W 73° 46.664'
P.M.   latitude N 83° 50.279'   longitude W 73° 51.159'
Distance traveled: 1 nm   Total nm from Ward Hunt: 45 nm
Hours traveled: 2 hrs.   Total nm to North Pole: 371 nm
Total hours traveled: 68 hrs.   Temperature: P.M. -33° C

We woke to a completely changed landscape, as if someone had done a scene change while we slept. The piles of ice blocks that stopped us yesterday were gone! Where they went to is a mystery. What appeared to be the end of the lead yesterday now stretched westward. Our lake-like lead was frozen over with a THIN skin of sparkling ice. The gloomy mist gave way to clear cold blue skies.

At -33° C, the ice on the lead did not freeze thick enough to support us. We continued along the west edge of the lead for two hours, skiing in a long line with pulks on a fully extended trace. Occasionally, we skied on short sections of "rubber ice" five- to six-centimeters thick. This ice was so thin that I could drive the tip of my ski pole tip through it, but thick enough that I couldn't pound the ski basket through.

If you like an adrenaline rush, skiing on rubber-ice is exhilarating. For poor Jan it was a nightmare. Sea ice is very elastic compared to brittle freshwater ice. As you ski it buckles under your weight and gives your stomach the sensation of walking on a trampoline or water bed.

We finally came to a point where the lead narrowed to 75 meters. The opposite shore looked so close! I toyed with the thought that if I skied fast I could make it to the other side. I debated...the sun made me feel optimistic; we were eager to push on—since the storm our mileage was more westerly than northerly. The Peter Pan in me wanted to zip across. But my intuition insisted that the risks were too high. No one's life is worth a couple of nautical miles.

I continued around the point at the narrows. The bank became higher and steeper. Not good, no escape route. I stopped to test the ice again, then swung out around a darker patch of thin ice. Jan skied right behind me. Claire followed. Around the point, we stepped off the thin ice onto a low pan to wait for the others. Claire mentioned, in an off-handed way, "I felt the ice give under me so I skied fast." As we waited, I wondered what could be taking so long. I unclipped from my pulk and climbed up the bank to have a look. Denise was just below me and called up that Ann had gone through and was clinging onto a ledge just below me. Unfortunately, Ann had been following the pulk tracks that cut the corner, not my ski tracks around the dark ice. When she felt the ice give under her, she managed to quickly leap to the bank and pull herself up on a small ledge. Clinging onto the ledge, she was out of sight from both those of us ahead and those behind. It was a few minutes before Denise and Sue, who were merrily chatting away, realized that Ann's pulk had not moved for some time. Denise unclipped from her pulk and with the throw-line rescue bag in hand, skied around the dark ice to find Ann perched on the side of the bank with one leg dangling in the water. Denise tossed her the throw-line and pulled first her pulk and then Ann across the thin ice along the edge of the steep bank. Ann explained later that she had refrained from calling out for help because she did not want to alarm anyone.

I am relieved that I listened to my intuition and did not attempt to cross the lead but feel badly that I led Ann into a cold bath along the edge of the lead. Ann assured us that she only needed to change her right boot liners. She is really an extraordinary woman. She had never done anything remotely like this in her life and yet her unplanned dip in the Arctic ocean did not upset her; she simply took it in stride.

We were now a well-rehearsed team with this wet foot drill: pre-warm dry socks next to body, de-ice laces with hot water, pull off boot, remove wet liner, replace with spare liner, put on dry socks, warm foot in parka of a friend, break ice off laces and pull on boot. As we performed this operation, the head of a seal popped up through the ice! What a surprise to see a living creature up here in this desolate, seemingly lifeless sea of ice. The ice must have been thin out on the lead for a seal to push up through it. In the back of my head lurked the uncomfortable thought that fat seals are the polar bears' favorite food. Where there are seals, there are polar bears, and where there are few seals, there will be hungry polar bears.

Decision time again. At the point where Ann went through, the lead widened and bent south. A very disheartening sight. When I am in doubt about making a decision,

I seek more information. This gives me time to check out my intuition and fully evaluate the situation and the group energy level. To recon our options and to re-warm Ann, we took a walkabout to check the route south around the lead. As far as we could see from the top of a ridge, there were large ice islands but no promise of a crossing. Not good. Our options were: to wait and hope that the lead freezes thicker by evening, or to ski south and look for an ice bridge. The group consensus was to set up camp, dry Ann out, and hope that the lead freezes enough to cross after dinner. Skiing into the night is now possible as we have 24 hours of light—not bright sunlight, but dusk.

It is depressing to be in the tent on such a fine traveling day. Held up again. Alpha's hopes of making the 84th parallel are slipping away. This is yet another test of our patience. Unless we want trouble, we must play by HER rules—the Goddess of the Sea, the Inuit's Sedna.

The story of Sedna has many variations across the High Arctic. The one that I tell is a composite of all my favorite parts pulled together.

Sedna was a beautiful young Inuit girl (maybe I added the beautiful, as all fairy-tale heroines are beautiful). She was a strong-minded young woman who frustrated her father by rejecting the suit of many good hunters. In Inuit society a daughter was a liability, as a father had to feed and clothe her for many years, only to give her to a husband. A son, on the other hand, was honor-bound to share his hunt with his parents. Having many sons was good life insurance and old age pension.

Anyway, back to Sedna, who continued to frustrate her father by refusing many good hunters. One day, a very handsome hunter came and promised Sedna the usual stuff that men have promised women for millennia: a beautiful igloo of thick white snow blocks, enough seal fat to light many kudliks (seal oil lamps), the finest fur clothes and caches full of seal, walrus, fish and caribou. Sedna, like women through millennia, allowed herself to believe him. She agreed to become his wife, to keep his igloo warm and scrape his skin clothes.

A few years later, Sedna's father was kayaking in the area and thought he'd drop by to visit Sedna. When Sedna saw her father, she rushed down the beach to meet him. "Father," she implored, "Take me away from here! My husband is not really a man. He is a Shaman and takes on the forms of animals. The snow of my igloo is rotten, my clothes are rags, and all that he feeds me is fish guts. Take me away!!"

Sedna's father jumped back into his kayak and quickly pushed off. He did not want to arouse the anger of a Shaman. Sedna, still a strong-minded woman, was not about to be left behind and jumped on the back of her father's kayak.

Meanwhile, Sedna's husband, in the form of a raven, swooped down and screamed out to Sedna's father, "Bring back my woman or I will make the seas rise and the waves send you to the bottom of the cold, dark sea." The raven swooped lower, the waves crashed higher over the deck of the little skin kayak. Finally, in a desperate attempt to save himself, Sedna's father whipped out his savik (hunter's knife) and lopped off Sedna's clutching fingers. Sedna sank to the bottom of the cold, dark sea.

But that was not the end of Sedna. According to legend, Sedna's fingers became the animals of the sea: the fish, the seals, the walrus and the whales. From that time ever after, when the hunting is poor, a Shaman must take up his drum and dance into a trance to descend down to the bottom of the cold, dark sea to find Sedna. To appease her, he has to comb and braid her long black hair. This releases the sea animals that are entangled in her hair and so ensures that the hunting will again be good.

Sedna can be good and bad; a Sea Goddess or a Sea Witch. She is not a spirit to trifle with. Crossing on her ice, we must play by her unwritten rules. Laugh at her jokes when she splits the ice between us or causes the pressure ridges to come alive under us.

I use Sedna to teach a humble attitude towards the Arctic. We cannot conquer the Arctic with our superior high-tech equipment or invincible attitudes. The Arctic cares nothing for us. We must listen to her moods.

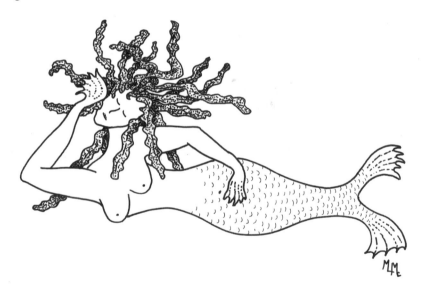

At 6:00 p.m., Denise and I put on our skis and headed out to test the lead. With Denise on the bank holding the throw-line bag ready, I skied out on the thin ice. A couple of meters out I stopped and bounced. The ice wobbled around me as if I was on a bowl of Jell-O. Oops; ever so gently I backed up. We tested a number of areas, chopping holes with the ice ax to check the ice thickness. As much as we were anxious to push on, Denise and I decided that the ice was still not thick enough to cross. We decided to go to bed early and set our alarm for 3:00 a.m.

The radio is down. No power. For just a second, Denise accidentally switched the positive and negative plug-ins. No sparks, no short-circuit smell...but now no power and changeover is in two days! Denise feels terrible. No one blames her. It was a mistake, no big deal, an additional challenge to our adventure. It is essential on a stressful expedition like this one that no one sink into blame or guilt. We must not dwell on the "should have," "what if," or "I wish we had." We cannot allow ourselves to get dragged down by negative thoughts or events that we are powerless to change. We need all our collective positive energy to move forward.

I wonder if anyone has ever studied how draining negative energy is or the amount of energy that it takes to motivate oneself to move into the unknown. Even at home it takes me more energy, not necessarily time, to follow a new recipe rather than one that I know.

Day 14 Alpha Day 14

MARCH 27, 1997

A.M.   latitude N 83° 50.526'   longitude W 73° 57.140'
P.M.   latitude N 83° 58.418'   longitude W 74° 08.678'
Distance traveled: 8 nm   Total nm from Ward Hunt: 53 nm
Hours traveled: 8 hrs.   Total nm to North Pole: 363 nm
Total hours traveled: 76 hrs.   Temperature: P.M. -40° C

Up at 3:00 a.m. and off by 6:00 a.m. The lead was frozen to a reassuring thickness. After a day-and-a-half of waiting, we crossed the narrows in less than five minutes. We skied along the curve of the lead as it widened and continued up a frozen tributary that headed north.

It was rather cold today, -33° C this morning with a drop to -40° C by the time we set up camp. I had a hard time keeping my face and fingers from freezing. Even in these temperatures I sweat profusely, which causes me to cool down at an alarming rate when we stop. In these conditions, there is no margin for error. As a last resort I pulled out my caribou mitts. Caribou is by far the warmest clothing that I have used in the Arctic. Caribou is super-warm and lightweight because of its hollow hair construction. The problem with caribou clothing is that it is very bulky, the hair is brittle and, if it gets wet, the skin dries stiff and must be scraped to soften and stretch it back into shape.

We have tried our best to reach the 84th degree of latitude. After eight hours of hard hauling we found a landing strip that was the best we had seen in a week. We are now a mere 1.5 nautical mile from 84° N!! So close.

Day 15 Alpha Day 15

MARCH 28, 1997

A.M.   latitude N 83° 58.299'   longitude W 74° 08.559'
P.M.   latitude N 83° 58.309'   longitude W 74° 08.200'
Distance traveled: 0 nm   Total nm from Ward Hunt: 53 nm

Hours traveled: 0 hrs.   *Total nm to North Pole: 363 nm*
Total hours traveled: 76 hrs.   *Temperature: P.M. -40° C*

Since the radio is still down, I got up at 5:30 a.m. to send an Argos message: "#0001, conditions excellent, good for changeover." At 7:30 p.m. I sent a second message "#1010, overcast, visibility good, strip marked, land on multi-year ice." Two hours later I sent the same message to indicate that conditions had not changed. At 2:00 p.m. the weather cleared and I changed the Argos back to "#0001, conditions excellent, good for changeover." It is frustrating not knowing if and when the plane is coming.

The Argos can send messages but not receive them. It is used daily to update our position with base in Resolute. It also serves as a back-up in case our radio breaks down or transmissions are disrupted. Every night I set a code on the Argos, attach the antenna, flip the "on" switch and set the Argos outside the tent. Every two hours a passing satellite picks up the signal and relays it to a communication center. Our support team in Resolute can access these messages from the communication center by e-mail. We have pre-arranged codes such as #0000 to mean "conditions OK, going well." This is the code I send most often. We have several codes for emergencies, such as #1111 "need to evacuate whole group ASAP." I hope never to use this one.

It's 3:00 p.m., the skies are clear, the runway marked and still no plane! We are going crazy...we could have gotten up early and traveled six to eight hours by now, and reached 84° N. Without a radio we can't guess what's happening. Emotions are running high. Are they coming today? Does Team Bravo need more time to get ready? Or was First Air called off to do a medical evacuation?

We sit, drinking tea, talking and looking to the south, ready to jump at the first sound of the plane. Denise and I took baths last night. Denise even washed her hair. I've repaired my ski bindings, dried and retied my pulk trace, and written to Paul and the children.

Day 16 Alpha Day 16

MARCH 29, 1997

A.M.   latitude N 83° 58.309'   longitude W 74° 08.200'
P.M.   latitude N 84° 01.229'   longitude W 74° 09.089'
Distance traveled: 2 nm   Total nm from Ward Hunt: 55 nm
Hours traveled: 4 hrs.   Total nm to North Pole: 361 nm
Total hours traveled: 80 hrs.   Temperature: P.M. -28° C

At 12:30 a.m. I woke to the sound of footsteps. They sounded very close to the tent. I sat up quickly. All sleeping bags were full, no one was out for a pee. "Crunch, crunch, crunch..." I shook Denise, "Denise, polar bear!" We were up in a flash. I decided to get dressed before dealing with the situation but Denise dove out the tunnel door in her long underwear to retrieve my gun. (The gun is kept outside to avoid condensation.) Between the crunch, crunch we heard voices. Oh, thought Denise, talking polar bears. With her head out the door, she called out in a surprised voice, "There are people out there!"

To the south, three human forms emerged out of the ice fog, crunch, crunch, crunch. They looked so far away yet sounded so close. Why weren't they pulling pulks? Were they in trouble? It must be the Polar Free team.

It was Polar Free. Scotty greeted me with a big grin and a frosty hug. They had followed our tracks thinking that we were the Dutch team until they recognized our big Weber tent. (They have a three-person mini Weber tent.) We stood and talked for a few minutes. Scotty asked, "What's the temperature? Our thermometer broke." "It's -38° C," we informed them. "Wow," Scotty exclaimed in surprise, "no wonder my nose and fingers are freezing." I didn't know about his fingers but his nose had been frozen and the other fellows had black, scabby cheeks. They had been on the trail for 12 hours and still had to return to shuttle their second load before setting up camp on the far side of our runway. We told them about our battery problems. Scotty offered to lend us their battery if we'd stop by their camp in about an hour when they were set up. This was extremely generous of them. They are an unsupported expedition and cannot, by their self-imposed rules, have new batteries sent in.

I was shivering when I got back into my sleeping bag. Two hours later Denise and I walked over to the Polar Free camp. We were invited to squeeze into their mini-tent. It was very small, about two meters in diameter, with a ski pole for a center pole. (In our tent we use a ski.) We shared what news we had of other expeditions and congratulated each other on how well we were doing. They informed us that David Hempleman-Adams had only 24 liters of fuel for their entire unsupported trip!! (We hauled 80 liters for the first 20 days!) I'm betting that David will be the next to burn out. Scotty lent us his battery and we said good night...although it was really 5:00 in the morning.

The reason that the Polar Free team were traveling so late at night is that they are on a 28-hour day. Their day consists of: three hours for breakfast and to break camp, 12 hours on the trail, four hours to make camp, melt water and eat dinner, nine hours of sleep. With 24 hours of light they roll their days to enable them to travel longer hours.

I was up again at 8:00 a.m. after only three hours of sleep. The weather had closed in. I sent Argos code #0010, "weather poor, re-supply/changeover not possible." We hooked up Scotty's battery. Bummer, their battery was dead. Our inability to communicate was really frustrating us. If we knew that the plane was not coming today we could make miles north. Sue, recalling her high school physics, began work on the radio. She taped four headlamp batteries in series and hooked them to the radio. It worked! We now could pick up a conversation between First Air and the Dutch about a resupply plane, but they did not mention our Bravo Team changeover. We were under the impression that we were splitting a charter with the Dutch team so Bravo should have been on the same plane. How frustrating not to be able to transmit!

At 2:00 p.m. Denise went back to talk to Scotty about their battery. Scotty thought it might be a blown fuse. He came by later with a new fuse and a voltmeter. They were to head off soon and we could use their fuse for one hour while they packed up.

Expectantly, we hooked up the Polar Free fuse and radioed in:

"Alpha Polar Relay, Alpha Polar Relay, do you copy?"

"This is Resolute, go ahead, Alpha Polar Relay."

Yes! We had contact with the outside world! We learned that team Bravo was in Eureka. They were on the plane ready to head north when they got our Argos code, "weather poor, re-supply/changeover not possible." We gave them a weather update, "snowing, light westerly winds, temperature rising to -28° C, visibility one kilometer." They will stand by for improved weather.

With the use of Scotty's voltmeter, Sue (a surgeon) and Claire (a chiropractor) dissected our battery pack despite the warning from Scotty not to open the individual batteries. Inside they found five rows of four- D size lithium batteries. Testing each battery revealed that one in each row had blown its internal fuse. Using duct tape and hair elastics, Sue and Claire regrouped the remaining good batteries.

"Yes! Yes! Yes! We have power" shouted Claire. Three cheers for Sue and Claire. We had enough power to receive clearly but our responses were garbled. We could answer with one click for "Negative" and two—click, click—for "Roger Roger." First Air asked:

"Is the weather improving?" click

"Do you have adequate food?" click, click

"Is the runway marked?" click, click

"Is the visibility less than 1 mile?" click, click

But they failed to inform us of what was going on. When will they come?!! It was frustrating that we could not ask questions.

The weather continued to be poor. Every half-hour we turned the radio on. At 5:00 p.m. First Air said they would not come today. "We will try again tomorrow," was their reply. In an excited rush, we gulped down dinner and packed up. Finally, we knew that they were not coming and could make miles.

Across the runway, the Polar Free Team advanced to meet us and collect their battery. We took photos, offered a round of handshakes and good luck wishes. I do hope they make it. They have 51 days of food left, and hope to make the Pole by May 20.

They repacked this afternoon, to get their kit into one pulk and one backpack per person, in the hopes that they can now haul single loads and not have to return for a second load.

Onward we marched, northward to the 84th. After two hours of walking due north, we felt sure that we had passed the 84th meridian and started to look for a runway. Visibility was less then 1/2 mile and there was little definition. We paced out four possibilities, but in the flat lighting, distances were deceiving. We finally came to a large pan that offered a number of options and decided to make camp and mark a runway when the light improved.

Day 17 Alpha Day 17

MARCH 30, 1997

A.M.   latitude N 84° 01.229'   longitude W 74° 09.089'
P.M.   latitude N 84° 02.283'   longitude W 73° 59.707'
Distance traveled: 1 nm   Total nm from Ward Hunt: 56 nm
Hours traveled: 2 hrs.   Total nm to North Pole: 360 nm
Total hours traveled: 82 hrs.   Temperature: P.M. -30° C

At 5:00 a.m. I sent the Argos code #0001, "conditions excellent; good for changeover," and crawled back into my sleeping bag.

The morning dawned clear and bright. After breakfast Alpha Team marked off the runway while Denise and I took sponge baths and finished letters. We were slurping hot drinks when, at 12:30 p.m., we heard the plane. What a mad rush. Hot drinks were dumped, stoves shut down, and we all tried to pile out the door at the same time. Ann had tears of joy running down her face. As the plane circled, we dashed about, kicking snow off the snow flaps, taking photos and stuffing the tent in a pulk. The plane touched down to test the snow and lifted off. It circled to the west, dropped lower for a closer look, looped east, made a couple of passes, dropped out of sight and did not rise again. "She's down!" By radio they informed us that they were one nautical mile to the east. This was not what we had expected. Guess they didn't like our runway. We ran to our runway to collect the pulks and sleeping bags which had been used to mark the strip and set off as fast as we could across masses of ice rubble. While I was taking a compass bearing in the direction the plane went down, the group bolted off. Claire, off the starting line first, cut around an ice block and circled back towards camp. Ann headed off to the south. They finally waited for me to shoot the bearing and lead off. We traveled 30 minutes, then stopped to listen for the Twin Otter engines. (The pilots must leave the engines running when it's very cold.) No sound. On we scrambled; Sue wanted to go more left (north), Denise more right (south). I was beginning to have nightmares of looking for a needle in a haystack. From a high point Denise, with her eagle eyes, spotted the tail of the plane 1/2 mile due east, right on my compass bearing. Once the plane was spotted, the Alpha Team was off like rockets, leaving Denise and me, with our heavier pulks full of group gear, sprinting to keep up, sweat pouring down our backs. As we approached the plane, Team Bravo jumped out to greet us.

Changeover was a nightmare for me. Even with a down parka on, I could feel my body temperature rapidly dropping. Denise and I checked the Bravo pulks and discovered that they were set up for 20 days of food and fuel. I checked with Michael, who had flown in with Bravo to make sure that our first changeover went smoothly, as to why we had 20 days of food. Bravo was only scheduled to go out for 12 days. With three spare (emergency) days of food, they should have had 15 days of food. We quickly sorted through the pulks and took out the extra five days of food and fuel.

By the time I climbed into the icy cold belly of the Twin Otter, I was extremely cold. To change into my clean resupply clothes, I had to strip down, totally naked. I began to shiver uncontrollably and my fingers became useless. I recognized that I was becoming dangerously hypothermic. I re-warmed my hands on the back of my neck, then hurried to get another layer of clothes on. Even fully re-dressed, I did not re-warm. I was unable to open the parcel from Paul, so in frustration I dumped the entire package in my pulk. Working out my film needs was also beyond me, so I took all of the film. I was stuck in slow motion. The pilots were getting concerned about burning up their return fuel. Outside (which seemed warmer than in the plane), I told Denise I was hypothermic and asked her to keep an eye on me. I went for a quick jog. As I jogged down the runway I started to cry; I wanted to go home, I was tired of being cold, I wanted a hot shower, to wash my hair, to be with my family. I knew that some of these feelings had rubbed off from the departing Alpha group talking of home and reuniting with their families and friends.

Back from my re-warming run, Denise and I rechecked that we had six pairs of skis and poles (not more or less), a new tent, new radio batteries, the corrected quantities of food and fuel for 15 days, and that everyone had: a sleeping bag system, expedition parka, extra clothes and no extra toys. The pilots were anxious to be off. There was a final round of good-bye hugs, the plane door was secured shut and the engines revved up. The plane lumbered over the snow, turned and, with a tremendous roar of power, the Twin Otter bounced over the snow and lifted off.

Part of me left with Ann, Claire, Sue and Jan. I was really going to miss those women! Over the last 17 days we had become so close. Facing and overcoming challenges had unified us into an efficient team and our laughter and talks in the tent had bonded our friendship. I hope our friendship will continue over the years and not be limited to these weeks on the ice.

The Twin Otter took off with Team Alfa, leaving me with a low heart and 360 nautical miles to go. My teammates were gone and in their place stood four strangers. At first I could not recognize which name went with which body as everyone was dressed in red suits with fur-hooded ruffs, neck warmers that covered their lower face and goggles with a nose guard covering the upper face. Rose is the tall one, Karen is broad in the beam, Catherine lumbers like a bear and by process of elimination, Emma is the other one.

Denise and I welcomed the group with, "We can offer no guarantees other than this will be an experience that you will never forget. We have many miles ahead of us, so let's strap our skis on and head to the North Pole. Later, when we set up our camp, we will review camp duties and, around hot drinks, get to know each other. For now I will lead and Denise will bring up the rear."

Unfortunately, after two hours it was necessary to call a stop. The Bravo women had not eaten or had anything to drink since leaving Eureka this morning. Their trail lunch-snacks were packed deep in their pulks and their water bottles were frozen, having spent the night on the plane. This was not a good way to start.

Denise and I introduced the group to the camp routines developed by the last team. Catherine volunteered to help me with stoves, as her hands get cold quickly. Karen offered to assist Denise with setting up the radio wires. That left Rose and Emma to shovel snow around the base of the tent to secure the snow flap.

In less than ten minutes the tent was up. Catherine and I crawled in and fired up the four stoves, emptied water from my water bottles into the pots and started melting snow. (If water is not put into the pot of snow, the bottom scorches before the snow starts to melt, giving a burnt metallic taste to the water.) When Emma and Rose finished shoveling snow on the snow flap, they started handing in sleeping systems and personal stuff sacs. Catherine and I arranged the rolled-up sleeping systems around the outer walls like backless easy chairs. Everyone was assigned to a specific place inside the tent, starting to the left of the entrance: #1, #2, #3 and #4. I am at #5 (my good luck number) and Denise is #6. Number 7 is where the radio is set up and stoves, pots and food are stacked at night, and the tunnel door is #8.

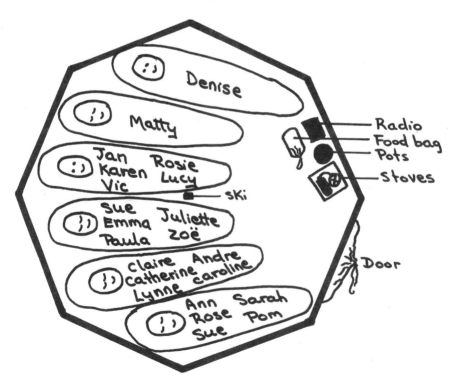

By the time the outside folks came in and tied the door closed, the water was ready for a first round of hot drinks. Over hot drinks Denise and I introduced the inside duties they would share: melting snow, cooking dinner, cleaning dinner dishes and writing in the group journal. We asked the team what rotation system they wanted to use. There was a suggestion to rotate by position in the tent, #1 melt snow, #2 cook dinner, #3 clean up dinner, #4 write in the group journal. Tomorrow #1 will cook dinner, #2 clean up dinner, etc.

During soup with melted cheese chunks and a second round of hot drinks, the usual getting-to-know-you questions were tossed about. Rose Agnew is 51. She was born in Germany, married a Brit and, for 25 years, has lived in London. She has three grown children and teaches at a girls' comprehensive school. She is the oldest Polar Relay expedition member.

Catherine Clubb is 28, single and lives in West Yorkshire. She works as an outdoor instructor teaching rock climbing, hiking, navigation and kayaking.

At 21 years old, Emma Scott is the "baby" of the expedition. She has earned a Gold Duke of Edinburgh Award and is a student at Plymouth, studying Recreation.

Karen Bradburn, age 37, lives in Kincardineshire (outer London) with her husband. She has seen much of the world through her job as a flight attendant. Karen and Emma have already become great chums.

Denise and I were torn between focusing on getting to know this group and digging into our packages from friends and family. So, after the initial round of questions, I opened the large package from Paul, which included letters from Eric and Sarah. Eric said that homeschool is going well, that he has been out lots with the dogs and that his budgies are happy. Sarah said, "I'm fine, how are you doing?" She has sent a couple of lateral thinking problems. I shared one with the group: "Mr. and Mrs. Brown have five children. If half of their children are girls, what are the other half?" Paul sent a long letter about how hard it was for him not to be in Resolute to offer me support during my stressful time there. He wrote that Sarah had a good report card, mostly As and Bs, that Eric is working on a major solar energy project, and provided an update on our NorthWinds dog sledding programs. My home support team, Paul, Eric and Sarah, have included a bag of beef jerky and a big box of chocolate. Not keen to haul extra weight, I passed the chocolate around for dessert.

It is a huge relief to know that all is well at home. But news from family emotionally pulls me away from my focus here. I find it draining to be pulled in two directions.

Day 18 Bravo Day 1

MARCH 31, 1997

A.M.   latitude N 84° 02.301'   longitude W 73° 59.551'
P.M.   latitude N 84° 07.701'   longitude W 74° 02.462'
Distance traveled: 6 nm   Total nm from Ward Hunt: 62 nm
Hours traveled: 7 hrs.   Total nm to North Pole: 354 nm
Total hours traveled: 89 hrs.   Temperature: P.M. -37° C

"6:30 Rise and Shine!" This has become my morning call to start the day.

This group didn't seem so keen to leave the warmth of the tent this morning, especially when I told them it was a cold -37° C, with a nasty west wind. By 9:30 a.m. we were off like a herd of turtles. North...north...north, always and forever north. (My mental jingle for the day.)

More of the same scenery: ice chunks, snow dunes, endless mounds and ridges of snow and ice. To deflect the boredom, I watched my shadow jump over the snow as it raced along to keep up with me. In the morning it was on my left. At noon I could ski on my shadow and by afternoon it traveled along on my right. When I get really bored, I work out calculations in my head...if we average five nautical miles a day it will take another 72 days...if we can push it to six nautical miles, it will only be 60 more days.... Today I also made a mental list of all that I'd do differently if I ever was crazy enough to participate in a similar expedition again. My journal is not large enough to write the entire list but at the top is: insist on being more involved through the initial preparations, participate in the selection of participants, have time to develop trust and respect with the expedition support team (Pen, Caroline, Mike, Nobby, and Geoff) and allow a full year to test clothing and equipment.

Today we skied a long seven hours and gained a good six nautical miles. This is better than I expected for Bravo's first full day "in harness." I worry that they may have been overly keen today and might not have the same bounce tomorrow. My initial impressions of this group is that they will be a good group. Our first travel day and mileage north was rewarding, camp set up was efficient and there was lots of laughter in the tent. I am still struggling to emotionally let go of the last group and embrace this new team.

Over dinner I shared the answer to Sarah's lateral thinking problem: If Mr. and Mrs. Brown had five children and half of them were girls, what was the other half? GIRLS!

Day 19 Bravo Day 2

APRIL 1, 1997

A.M.   latitude N 84° 07.675'   longitude W 74° 02.131'
P.M.   latitude N 84° 12.188'   longitude W 74° 09.299'
Distance traveled: 4 nm   Total nm from Ward Hunt: 66 nm

Hours traveled: 6.5 hrs.   *Total nm to North Pole: 350 nm*
Total hours traveled: 95.5 hrs.   *Temperature: P.M. -33° C*

Slower going today. I'm afraid Denise and I pushed the group too hard yesterday or rather we let them travel too long. As we had feared, they did not have much bounce today. If this group is made up of the "Second Big Guns," according to Pen, I worry about how strong the other groups will be.

Sometime in the afternoon I pulled a muscle in my groin. As the day wore on the pain increased. My poles became crutches and I shuffled along on my skis. The pain was draining. When I got to camp and took my skis off, the pain was so extreme that I could not lift my leg. To take a step, I had to grab a handful of pant material and lift. "Mustn't grumble."

This evening I decided to resort to drugs for the pain. I have a strong aversion to drugs, in any form. My belief stems from my father's conviction that drugs merely camouflage the pain so that you fail to take care of yourself. As he explained to me when I was a kid, if you have a head cold and take drugs, you will feel better and, instead of putting your body to bed, you will continue to run yourself down. Or if you pull a muscle and use drugs to alleviate the pain you might continue to use the muscle, doing more damage and prolonging your recovery. But earlier this evening the pain was excruciating and draining my energy so I took a couple of painkillers. The Brits do have some good ones and after dinner I wasn't feeling any pain.

Day 20 Bravo Day 3

APRIL 2, 1997

A.M.   latitude N 84° 12.158'   longitude W 74° 09.482'
P.M.   latitude N 84° 17.804'   longitude W 74° 14.084'
Distance traveled: 6 nm   Total nm from Ward Hunt: 72 nm
Hours traveled: 7 hrs.   Total nm to North Pole: 344 nm
Total hours traveled: 102.5 hrs.   Temperature: P.M. -33° C

This morning before dismantling our camp, we went through all the lunches and removed the peanuts and dried fruit that no one can eat. In total, we "gave Sedna" nine kilograms of lunch food! I hate throwing away calories but, even worse, I hate hauling food that we will not eat.

I should explain what we do with our garbage. This has been a hotly debated issue. Most people are under the illusion that they have done their environmental duty when they flush their waste down the toilet and put their garbage out to be picked up by the garbage truck. But where does the garbage go and does our responsibility stop there? How much can we recycle? How conscious are we about the amount of packaging we use? These are the questions I think one must come to terms with. In Resolute, garbage is hauled out to an archaic dump site and burned. What doesn't burn blows onto the tundra and into the sea. If we send our garbage back to Resolute, we are contributing to this problem. The tundra is a fragile environment and around the Resolute area it supports muskoxen, caribou, arctic wolf, fox, arctic hare, lemming and many migrating bird populations. The ocean around Resolute is abundant with whales, walrus, seals, fish and polar bears. My position for the expedition is for us to carry out our plastic bags so they can be washed and reused by the next group and to bury the rest of our garbage down cracks in the ice. When the ice shifts, our debris will be pulverized. There is no land under us and very few animals, so the effect of this garbage is minimal.

This morning, we traveled in a maze of old leads and refrozen ice rubble. The ice rubble resembled the shape of giant frosted heads of cauliflower. It made for some awkward balancing acts as our skis skidded off in unpredictable directions. In the afternoon we came to a new arrangement of pressure ridges. The ice blocks were piled up like stone walls 20- to 40-centimeters thick. Their clean right-angle fractures contrasted sharply to the random, rounded piles of earlier ice rubble. They seemed newly sculpted and their edges not yet softened by melting sun and sand-blasting winds.

The symmetry of shadows caused by the low sun is arctic art. I wish that I were able to capture the colors of light in a watercolor painting: the ultra-marine blues and emerald greens changing to cold cobalt blue. The light is always changing. We find ourselves skiing through a world of flat pastel pinks and lavender and then, imperceptibly, the ambiance changes to a sharp intense blue with deep shadows.

We put in 6.5 hours to gain six nautical miles, an average day.

Day 21 Bravo Day 4

APRIL 3, 1997

A.M.	latitude N 84° 17.327'	longitude W 74° 15.817'
P.M.	latitude N 84° 24.599'	longitude W 74° 06.492'
Distance traveled: 7 nm		Total nm from Ward Hunt: 79 nm
Hours traveled: 7 hrs.		Total nm to North Pole: 337 nm
Total hours traveled: 109.5 hrs.		Temperature: P.M. -27° C

Another long, long day. A bit more gratifying than yesterday since we managed seven miles in seven hours. It still seems crazy that we can only average, on a good day, 1 nautical mile per hour. (One nautical mile is equal to 1.85 kilometers or 1.14 statute miles. I think of seven nautical miles as just shy of 14 kilometers or as a long 7 regular [statute] miles.) Back home I usually can average 5 kilometers an hour hiking and up to ten skiing. I have even skied 65 kilometers in one day! In comparison to these figures, our rate of progress is unbearably slow. It would be interesting to calculate the actual mileage that we are covering over the ice instead of our miles gained, as the crow flies, due north as indicated by our GPS. I am sure that some days our actual mileage is nearly double our miles gained, what with all the climbs over pressure ridges and zigzagging around leads.

We had an interesting event today. We were making good mileage across an old, lake-size, re-frozen lead when our progress was blocked by a small open lead. Following the lead westward, I found a place where a couple of floating ice blocks had rafted together to form a bridge. Rose and I cautiously crossed over. By the time Catherine came to cross, the lead had deceptively widened. It took Catherine a couple of seconds to comprehend why, with her long legs, she couldn't follow us. We continued westward on opposite banks for another half-hour until we found a narrows for the others to cross.

I am having breakthrough bleeding. It seemed like a great solution to go on the Pill, skipping the last week of empty estrogen pills to avoid having a period during the expedition. This worked for me in 1990 on the Baffin Island Expedition, a four-month dog-sledding journey. But up here, all of us who are on the Pill are having breakthrough bleeding. The worst is that we are unprepared. Using spare socks is the most common solution. Tonight on the radio call, I requested tampons for the next resupply.

Day 22 Bravo Day 5

APRIL 4, 1997

A.M.	latitude N 84° 24.366'	longitude W 74° 06.451'
P.M.	latitude N 84° 30.606'	longitude W 74° 13.869'
Distance traveled: 6 nm		Total nm from Ward Hunt: 85 nm
Hours traveled: 7 hrs.		Total nm to North Pole: 331 nm
Total hours traveled: 116.5 hrs.		Temperature: P.M. -37° C

"It's been a long hard day, and I've been working like a dog." My theme song for the day. This hauling pulks is for the dogs! I thought that the Amundsen-Scott race to the South Pole in 1911 had taught the Brits that dog travel was superior to man-hauling sledges. Roland Huntford expressed it so well in his book on Scott and Amundsen, when he said:

Scott was a heroic bungler. He added nothing to the technique of Polar travel, unless it was to emphasize the grotesque futility of man-hauling. As Helmer Hanssen put it: "What shall one say of Scott and his companions who were their own sled dogs?. . . I don't think anyone will ever copy him."

Helmer Hanssen was part of Amundsen's South Pole party.

For three weeks the pressure ridges have run across our direction of travel, snaking east to west. For the last two days they have been oriented northwest to southeast. I wonder if the pressure ridges originally formed east-west and have been turned, counter-clockwise, by stronger easterly ocean currents to the north of us.

It was a cold -37° C, making the snow very abrasive. It felt as if we were pulling 150 kilogram pulks across the sand. We worked seven hours to gain six miles.

After five days of skiing, Bravo Team's Uni-Flex bindings are starting to fail! Bravo brought in new skis mounted with new bindings so they have only used their skis for the ten-day training in Resolute and these last five days on the ice. (Alpha Team only skied two to three days because the snow was hard packed and the conditions so difficult.) It concerns me that we are encountering binding problems so soon. The screws keep loosening on several pairs of bindings every day. Today I snapped the metal toe bail on my binding. According to Richard Bentley, who manufactures these bindings, "You'll never break the bails. I've only heard of a broken one in 20 years." I was so confident in his words that I failed to bring spare bails. It's a bitch skiing with bindings strapped on with extra webbing and string.

We saw fox tracks 85 nautical miles from land! What does he eat? Seal carcasses left over by a polar bear? My rifle is always strapped to the top of my pulk and I often glance back over my shoulder to scan the ice rubble. When I ski at the end of the line, I glance back more often. Images of bears stalking us send prickles up my spine. I've heard stories of bears, on their silent furry pads, sneaking up and nabbing the person at the end of the line. The bears calculate that animals straggling at the back of the pack are the weakest and can be killed before the remainder of the herd is aware of an attack. I have rehearsed many times in my mind exactly what I will do if a bear is spotted: instruct the group to quickly come to me, tell Denise to keep the group behind me, pull the rifle out of its padded case, draw the bolt back, push the first cartridge into the chamber and keep the bear in my sights. I will watch a bear to ascertain if it is a curious bear just checking us out or a bear that is clearly going to charge. Up here on the polar ice, I've been warned to "shoot any bear that comes within range as there is little food for the bears and they are extremely dangerous." At 100 meters I'm a good shot and, at 50 meters, I can fire four fast rounds and put all within a ten-centimeter circle. My grandpa, Professor Malcom P. McNair of the Harvard Business School, taught me how to shoot when I was a young girl and I have his prized Winchester, Model 70 rifle with me. I have never had to shoot a polar bear and hope that I never am compelled to.

The Dutch are at 84° 46'. This places them 16 nautical miles north of us! David Hempleman-Adams and Rune are at 83° 30'. We were at this latitude on March 20, our Day 7. They started 10 days ahead of us. If this is their correct location, we are now 60 nautical miles ahead of them. I wonder what kind of difficulties David and Rune are having.

--- *Day 23 Bravo Day 6* ---

APRIL 5, 1997

A.M.   latitude N 84° 30.530'   longitude W 74° 13.236'
P.M.   latitude N 84° 36.606'   longitude W 74° 00.879'
Distance traveled: 6 nm   Total nm from Ward Hunt: 91 nm

Another day at the office: -27° C in the morning and -37° C when we made camp. Not an easy day to keep hands warm and functional. Catherine continues to have trouble maintaining circulation in her hands. After breaks is when her hands get dangerously cold and are difficult to re-warm. Cold hands are most frequently caused by capillary shunt at the extremities. This is our bodies' survival tactic to compensate for a drop in core temperature. To protect the vital organs, our bodies shut down the returning cold blood from the skin surface and the extremities. So Catherine's cold hands may mean that she is losing too much body heat and needs to add more clothing. Today I recommended she wear an extra pair of warm-up pants, and, after our breaks, I took her ski poles so she could swing her arms while skiing to force the blood to return to her fingers.

I led all day: north-northwest, north-northeast, north, north-northwest, north-northeast... depending on the route of least resistance. No drugs today; my pulled groin muscle has recovered. We had a little excitement today while crossing a lead. When we came to a ten-meter wide open lead, I turned west in search of a crossing. Not far along I came to a point where the two banks came closer together and pressurized all the ice debris into a solid mass. There was a deafening grinding and squeaking sound as the two plates of ice moved in opposite directions. I stood to observe and assess the motion of the ice. It was an odd sensation; I couldn't tell which bank was moving—was the opposite bank moving right or were we moving left? Even though the ice was moving slowly, the ominous cries of the ice got the adrenaline zipping. I decided that as long as the pressure continued to force the ice debris together, it was safe to cross. Karen, like Jan on the Alpha team, was very fearful of falling in, so she followed right behind me. Halfway across, the nose of Karen's pulk slid into a crack. Karen panicked and started screaming. "Karen, it's okay, you are on solid ice," I prompted as I unclipped from my pulk and went back to her. My words had no effect. I grabbed her arm to steady her and reassured her again, "You are okay, your pulk will float, stop screaming and let's get you to the other side. I am unclipping your pulk. Take a step." Holding her arm, I guided her to the far bank. Karen was trembling with fright and overwhelmed by embarrassment that she had panicked and lost her self-control. We all felt for her and gave her hugs and reassured her.

In the warmth of the tent, after a bowl of soup and a hot drink, I fill out the small black Captain's Log Book. Every night I record:

–date	–A.M. and P.M. latitude and longitude
–drift	–temperature
–wind speed and direction	–ice conditions
–nautical miles gained today	–nautical miles to north pole
–team morale	–medical incidents

I've discovered that if I ask for input on team morale before soup and hot drinks, it is lower than when I ask for it after. In true British form, low is stated as "good," or "not bad." If the GPS has given us better than expected mileage for the day, the collective group morale instantly swings up to "excellent!" "splendid!" or "brilliant!" Since this is not a true reflection of how the day was for individual team members, I have started requesting personal input from everyone. Tonight, for Emma, the 21-year-old student and youngest relay member, it was "a head-down day." Catherine, the outdoor instructor, found it "so draining to be so cold." Rose, the oldest member, said, "I had ups in the variety of terrain and downs when I kept falling in the ice blocks." Karen, the flight attendant, declared, "I feel good, could have gone on." Denise had "a cold foot day." And for me it was "just another day at the office."

Day 24 Bravo Day 7

APRIL 6, 1997

A.M.	latitude N 84° 36.628'	longitude W 74° 00.904'
P.M.	latitude N 84° 45.209'	longitude W 74° 00.358'
Distance traveled: 9 nm		Total nm from Ward Hunt: 100 nm
Hours traveled: 8 hrs.		Total nm to North Pole: 316 nm
Total hours traveled: 132 hrs.		Temperature: P.M. -35° C

A record-breaking nine nautical miles north in eight hours! This sure brings up the team morale. They are feeling "brilliant" and "spot on." The expedition is now 100 nm from Ward Hunt; the worst of the rough ice should (I hope) be behind us. We are in a celebrating party mood tonight. We raised our mugs of hot chocolate and toasted our success. And, not to forget, our thanks to Sedna, the Inuit spirit of the sea.

Life on the ice is good but I'm too tired to write more tonight.

Day 25 Bravo Day 8

APRIL 7, 1997

A.M.	latitude N 84° 45.271'	longitude W 73° 59.313'
P.M.	latitude N 84° 53.139'	longitude W 73° 58.953'
Distance traveled: 8 nm		Total nm from Ward Hunt: 108 nm
Hours traveled: 8 hrs.		Total nm to North Pole: 308 nm
Total hours traveled: 140 hrs.		Temperature: P.M. -32° C

I woke to the sound of a freight train: cars bumping and clanging into each other, brakes screeching. When I went out for my morning pee, I scanned the ice in the direction the sounds reverberated from, but saw nothing move. There must of been a pressure ridge building much further to the northeast than the sounds implied. On this silent side of the planet the sound is frightful. For 25 days, Denise and I have not heard cars, sirens whining, dogs barking, birds chirping, the wind in the trees. The sounds of our world on the ice are the soft sounds of the wind blowing snow over the ice, the stove boiling water, the swish of clothing when we ski, the crunch of our footsteps.

I've been contemplating how the pressure ridges of rectangular ice blocks that we've encountered lately are formed. I have come to the conclusion that, perhaps a month ago, medium-size leads opened throughout this area. Over the weeks that followed there must have been minimal ice movement and the leads re-froze to a half a meter in thickness. Then, ocean currents applied pressure from the north and crushed the ice together. Caught between thick multi-year pans of ice, the weaker new ice cracked and buckled up into these ridges of turquoise-blue blocks.

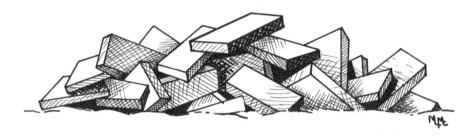

Karen had another scare today. Denise was leading across a newly refrozen lead and using a frozen large floater as a stepping stone. Emma followed. Karen was next but was very apprehensive. I moved up behind her and coached her, "Take your time, move slowly and keep your balance." I pulled her pulk up to ensure that it would not snag and held the rope taut to give her added support. Just as Karen stepped down on the floater, it broke through the thin new ice around it. With a shriek Karen jumped back and I provided a quick yank on her pulk rope. She landed back on the bank. It is amazing what a shot of adrenaline can do; Karen jumped backward, with skis on, up a half-meter bank. She even managed not to get her boots wet!! The rest of the team opted for a different route up and over a ridge of ice blocks.

As I waited for the others to climb up and over the ridge of ice blocks, I kept looking at the floating blocks of ice in the lead. I was captivated by the idea that, maybe, if I skied fast enough, I could zip across the floaters before they had time to sink. I was feeling a bit bored and the challenge was too titillating to deny. Zip! In less than two seconds I was across. It took the others another five minutes to climb over the ice blocks. When Karen arrived and saw me already on the other side, she wanted to know how I had gotten across ahead of her. I pointed to the lead of bobbing floaters. I felt a little guilty for taking the risk and for taking what for me was the easier way when the rest of the group had to struggle over a hill of ice chunks. (I must admit that I also felt smug and pleased with myself.)

There is lots of laughter in the tent tonight. We exploded with mirth, till we nearly wet our pants, reminiscing about how Karen skied off without her pulk after a snack break and didn't notice! It became more hilarious each time the story was retold.

Emma called out, "Oh, Karen, did you forget something?" Karen looked back, "What?" and Emma responded, "Are you planning on leaving your pulk here?"

After crossing the lead, the toe piece on my left ski binding snapped. Catherine also broke a bail in the afternoon. This worries me. I fear that the breaks are caused by metal fatigue and that more bails will break. Denise and I have discussed a number of solutions and agreed that we must obtain replacement bindings. We both want to switch to the Sherpa/Berwin bindings. This evening I explained the situation to Michael on the radio. I requested that he call Paul in Iqaluit, ask him to borrow the Berwin bindings belonging to the Outward Bound Society (I know that they are not using them this year) and ship them to Resolute to be mounted on the Charlie Team's skis. Michael seemed reluctant, voicing excuses like, "The expedition cannot afford additional expenses such as this one." I pointed out that we would borrow, not buy, the bindings. This interchange really infuriated me. How am I expected to get this expedition to the North Pole with the present ski binding problems? I felt discounted. Michael has no experience skiing and should acknowledge the 40 years of skiing experience I have. I had to insist that it was my decision and that I wanted the new bindings on the Charlie Team skis. He replied that he may not be able to get them in time for the next changeover. I instructed him to delay the changeover by a day if need be. Grrrrrr, growl, snarl…I felt that I had to fight to get what was needed, and to do it in front of the team. Now I am in a grumpy mood.

The tent is crowded with skis needing binding repairs. Time to put my journal aside and fix these bindings so we can roll out our sleeping systems and get to bed. I must remember to find my ear plugs, as this group is made up of four champion snorers!

Day 26 Bravo Day 9

APRIL 8, 1997

A.M.	latitude N 84° 53.121'	longitude W 73° 59.343'
P.M.	latitude N 85° 00.589'	longitude W 74° 07.777'
Distance traveled: 7 nm		Total nm from Ward Hunt: 115 nm
Hours traveled: 8 hrs.		Total nm to North Pole: 301 nm
Total hours traveled: 148 hrs.		Temperature: P.M. -32° C

We made the 85th degree of latitude! This puts us 5,100 nautical miles from the equator and 300 nautical miles from the North Pole! Plus we are back on the desired 74th meridian, which is due north of New York City.

At about 10:00 this morning, we came upon ski tracks running parallel to a lead. The tracks eventually crossed the lead and brought us to a camp with two tent rings. It must be the Dutch. We had heard that one of their members was evacuated because of back problems, so they are now down to two tents. We followed their trail until it turned east. Why, we wondered, did they turn east? We continued due north.

Tonight on the radio we heard that the Dutch position is at 85° 01'. If that is their latitude, we have gained on them and are only one nautical mile behind! Kohno is doing
well; he is at 86° 10'. The Polar Free are 16 nautical miles to the south of us at N 84°
44'. David is at 83° 56', 64 nautical miles south of us.

My bindings are driving me crazy. I can't take a step without watching my skis. With
my lashed-together bindings, my skis go every-which-way except the way my foot
is pointed. Every time I cross a pressure ridge, I have to put the bindings back together. It's a bummer limping along, and it's burning out my knees. Both Karen and Rose
are having problems with their binding screws continually loosening. I pray that
Michael gets the Berwin bindings to us.

We are now able to put in longer days on the trail. This group is a tad slow in the
morning, so we compensate by getting up at 6:00 a.m. This ensures that we eat
breakfast, pack up and are on our skis by 9:00 a.m. Eight hours on the trail (figuratively speaking, since there is no trail) puts us into camp at 5:00 p.m. By 5:45 p.m.
the tent is up and we are slurping soup with chunks of melted cheese. My first priority is to get my VBL (vapor barrier liner) socks off. Wet all day, my feet resemble
wrinkly albino prunes. I dry my polypropylene sock liners over a stove (I confess the
smell is not so appealing) and slip into my "après ski" slippers. This was Rose's brilliant idea to use our insulated water bottle jackets as slippers; these are feather-
weights compared to our heavy Sorel boots. Soup is followed by a hot drink, usually hot chocolate for me. Then it's time to turn on the GPS to get our miles du jour.
We call out our guesstimates as the GPS tracks satellites. I am consistently a conservative guesser. Suspense mounts. Blink, our present location is: N 85° 00.589' W
74° 07.777'. I press the GO TO button, scroll down to NORTH POLE and blink: 301
nautical miles. I subtract yesterday's miles-to-north-pole, and get seven nautical
miles! Yes, Denise wins again! It is uncanny how often she is "spot on." While water
bottles are being refilled and dinner bubbles, I fill out the Captain's Log Book, brush
my hair and strip down for a quick sponge bath. By the time my long underwear is
completely dried, it's dinner time. After another dinner of Harvest Foodworks (they
are all starting to taste the same), it's time to repair the daily collection of broken
bindings and scribble in our personal journals. After the radio call (on every other
day), we shut the stoves off and unroll the sleeping bag systems, three on each side
of the center pole (ski), with heads out and feet towards the door. "Lights out" at 9:00
p.m. is a joke since we now have 24 hours of bright light. To give me the illusion of
darkness and help me sleep, I pull my headband over my eyes.

─────────────── *Day 27 Bravo Day 10* ───────────────

APRIL 9, 1997

A.M.   *latitude N 85° 00.573'*   *longitude W 74° 07.611'*
P.M.   *latitude N 85° 07.823'*   *longitude W 74° 18.900'*
Distance traveled: 7 nm   *Total nm from Ward Hunt: 122 nm*

Hours traveled: 8.5 hrs.   *Total nm to North Pole: 294 nm*
Total hours traveled: 156.5 hrs.   *Temperature: P.M. -25° C*

We had a Biblical experience today. An hour out we were stopped by a wide lead cutting east-west. We traveled west along the lead, searching for a bridge or narrows. After about two kilometers, the lead turned south. With sinking hearts we stopped. To the south, the red mist rose as far as our eyes could see. Now what? Going west at least compensated for any easterly drift, but skiing south canceled hard-won miles north. We stood at the bend, gazing across five meters of black water. Then a miracle happened! Along the far shore the water began to ripple and ever so slowly the far shore slid towards us. In less than ten minutes, the far shore joined together right at our feet. It was awesome—just as impressive as the story of the Red Sea in the Bible. A spiritual experience for us all.

The Bravo members are becoming the "Wild Women skiers of the Arctic." This morning, kamikaze skier Emma led us over a 6 meter drop. With our pulk traces fully extended, we could defy gravity and walk straight down the drop. Our pulks acted as a counterbalance: as we slowly descended down one side of the ridge, we pulled our pulks up the other side. It was a wonderful sensation to walk down the incline, leaning straight out. This is fun until your pulk snags and you are left helpless and unable to reverse up the steep slope. Denise was the last one over Emma's route. To avoid having her pulk snag while she descended, she hand-over-hand hauled it up to the top of the ridge. Without the counterbalance, her descent was rapid, ending in a crash as she dramatically flew off a three-meter overhang. Her pulk descended and picked up speed as it plunged after her. Luckily she kept her head and ducked as her pulk shot over her. I wish I could have caught the stunt on film. Needless to say, Denise was not up for a rerun.

Karen snapped the toe bail on her left binding. To add to her troubles, the front screw on her right binding pulled out and both back screws were already stripped. I tightened the back screws by filling the screw holes with wooden match sticks and screwing them down again. Not much could be done with the front screw. I tried wrapping a cord around the binding and ski. It is not great but I hope it will hold for one more day.

―――――――――― *Day 28 Bravo Day 11* ――――――――――

APRIL 10, 1997

A.M.   latitude N 85° 08.087'   *longitude W 74° 11.614'*
P.M.   latitude N 85° 10.988'   *longitude W 74° 21.951'*
Distance traveled: 4 nm   *Total nm from Ward Hunt: 126 nm*
Hours traveled: 5 hrs.   *Total nm to North Pole: 290 nm*
Total hours traveled: 161.5 hrs.   *Temperature: P.M. -26° C*

What a day to look for a runway. After leaving camp, we followed along the rubbery shores of a lead that soon opened out into a horizonless lake. We made an about face back to our camp and continued east with the hopes of finding a crossing in a rubble zone. Once again the lead closed for us. But, just as we started to cross, it began to open. What a scramble! Denise, sinking in slush, slid backwards until her bindings were in the water. Concentrating to find a stable placement for her poles, she pushed herself and carefully climbed out on the far bank. Rose was the last to cross. By the time she started, the crack was nearly as wide as the length of her skis. Bravely, she stepped across. The center of her ski dipped in the water. I extended my ski pole to her; all of us held our breath as Rose was focused on moving methodically across. All this as the banks continued to slide apart. There was a great sigh of relief when she stepped up the steep shore. A cheer went up, "Wow, Rose, that was brave!" She explained, "There was no way I was going to be left alone on the far bank!"

We now entered an endless maze of open and moving leads. I was beginning to have serious doubts about finding a campsite, let alone locating a half-kilometer landing strip. At 2:00 p.m. we emerged from the maze of leads to find an enormous flat pan to the east! Perfect, what luck!

We paced out the runway. It was well over the minimum length and unusually flat. The pilots require a landing strip that is a minimum of 400 meters long and 50 meters wide. The runway must be aligned with the predominant winds so that the undulating snow dunes run parallel to the landing and, as much as possible, avoid cross-winds when landing. The surface must not have hard packed ridges of more than 10 centimeters high. They want to know how high the pressure ridges are at either end of the runway; if the ridges are low, they can use the entire runway. When the ridges are high, they must come in high and will need a longer landing strip. The runway most dreamed of by veteran arctic pilots is an old refrozen lead: long, smooth and flat. In four weeks of travel, I have seen only one that fits this description. To help me imagine what it would be like to land a plane on our chosen runway, I try to visualize how it would feel to drive a car down the runway at 120 kph.

In high spirits we set up camp, strung out the radio wires and called in the good news to Resolute. After soup and hot drinks, we fixed our hair and, looking our very best, stepped out to take group photos. Denise and I clicked Team Bravo group photos with everyone's cameras. "Wait, wait, one more! Smile!" Then I set the cameras up on ice blocks and, with self-timers on, snapped shots of all of us; jubilant adventurers of the Arctic. Karen wanted video shots of the team hauling pulks over ice rubble so Emma and Catherine put on their pulk harnesses and demonstrated sea ice mountaineering with skis and pulks. I also wanted to get individual portraits using a fill-in flash on backlit faces framed in fur hoods.

We were chilled by the time we crawled back into the tent and fired up the stoves again. I never leave stoves on unattended. If a stove were to flare up and start a tent fire, we would lose everything—tent, stoves, sleeping bags, radio, Argos, extra clothing...everything, except our pulks with some extra food and fuel in them. We would not be able to give our location and our chances of surviving more than a couple of days would be negligible.

A couple of us brought our cameras into the tent to get inside photos of our life inside our humble abode. Before bringing our cameras into the humid interior climate of the tent, we sealed them in plastic bags and hung them from the top of the tent until they reached the equivalent inside temperature. This ensured that when we took our cameras out of the plastic bags, they would not be covered with condensation. Cameras don't mind going from warm to cold. What damages a camera is going from cold to warm. The warm air holds more humidity and this condenses on cold objects. (If you wear glasses in a cold environment, you are familiar with this.) It is the equivalent of bringing your camera into a sauna. To make matters worse, the next time you expose your camera to cold temperatures, the moisture freezes, making moving mechanized parts inoperable.

The women were all told not to bring good cameras because they were too heavy and would probably be damaged or would fail to work in the extreme cold. Kodak gave the expedition a number of Advantex cameras and a few women brought small Instamatics. Denise and I both have good cameras. Denise chose a Nikon that is not very battery dependent: no auto advance or rewind. My camera is a Canon EOS A2 with a Tamron 28 to 200 zoom lens. (Weight of camera with lens is 1.3 kilograms.) I chose a zoom to avoid the difficulty of changing lenses with blowing snow and cold fingers. At the beginning of the expedition, I wore my camera under my wind jacket to keep the batteries warm with my body heat. The camera was placed in a coated nylon (waterproof) sac to keep perspiration from collecting on it. This allowed me to quickly access my camera, but the cold lump on my chest was awkward under my pulk harness. I now keep my camera nestled in the front of my pulk, tucked into my down parka with my two water bottles. The water bottle jackets leak enough heat to keep the camera batteries warm. So far both Denise's and my cameras seem to be functioning well. I say seem since we have not seen any results yet.

Day 29 Bravo Day 12

APRIL 11, 1997

A.M.   latitude N 85° 10.316'   longitude W 74° 27.501'
P.M.   latitude N 85° 10.175'   longitude W 74° 25.600'
Distance traveled: 0 nm   Total nm from Ward Hunt: 126 nm
Hours traveled: 0 hrs.   Total nm to North Pole: 290 nm
Total hours traveled: 161.5 hrs.   Temperature: P.M. -25° C

A.M. Clear day, good for changeover. What a luxury to sleep in, but after ten hours I couldn't hold my bladder any longer. I had to get out of my warm sleeping bag. Now back inside my warm cocoon, I am writing in my journal. Denise is busy making our mugs of coffee. I am always touched by the care with which she takes to make me coffee every morning. We are going to burn up some of our extra fuel by melting enough snow for Denise to wash and rinse her hair and for me to wash my long underwear so I can avoid stripping naked in the plane to change into clean underwear. There is something symbolic about washing away the sweat and stink to start fresh for the next relay.

P.M. Melting water, washing and marking the runway took up most of the morning. The afternoon was spent catching up in our journals. Denise is keeping a log of British terms like "bollocks" or "dogs' bollacks," which Catherine explained means dogs' balls and not proper to use in the company of the Queen. Emma and Karen were in a silly mood, teasing and joking with everyone. I read over the group journal. It was not very revealing or exciting. Except for the sections written by Rose in her gracefully flowing script that eloquently expressed the awesome magic of the Arctic, the rest was rather boring. Most entries give factual information, like how many miles north per day, the temperature, our geographic location, and how many hours we hauled. Not much in the way of emotional disclosures or insights. But then, this is a group journal that will be handed to Caroline at the end of the expedition and she plans to write a book.

As the day slipped away with no word or sound of a plane, our emotional moods also slipped from a top-of-the-world high to a depressing, confused, frustrated low. There must be bad weather to the south of us. At 6:00 p.m. First Air informed us that they would not fly at night. We don't understand: there are 24 hours of light up here. We radioed Michael at our Base and asked him why, with 24 hours of light, did First Air not want to fly at night? He must have confronted them on this because at 8:15 we learned that Team Charlie was finally on their way to Eureka. At 11:30 p.m. First Air told us they were leaving Eureka and requested a weather up-date every hour. So far, weather continues to be clear and holding.

I don't feel like writing much tonight. I drew a little cartoon of six stick figures pulling pulks across the top of the page. I showed my sketch to Karen. She got such a tickle out of it that I drew the same drawing in her journal...then in Denise's and Emma's journals.

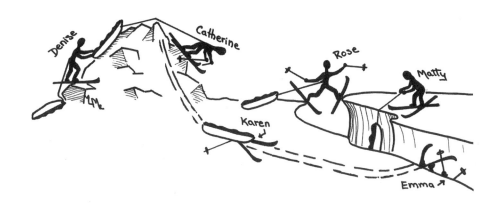

Day 30 Bravo Day 13

APRIL 12, 1997

At 1:30 a.m. I woke everyone up for hot drinks and breakfast. There was a thin haze of ice fog with visibility still at two to three kilometers. By 3:00 a.m. it was hard to see the end of the runway. At 3:15 a.m. we heard the Twin Otter pass overhead. Visibility was so poor that they could not see us. I radioed the pilots to let them know that they had just passed over head and gave them an update on our GPS location. We heard the plane circle again and again. By radio I gave them our location, "You are just west of us." "You are east of us." "You are over the runway." "You are at the east end of the runway." "You are at the west end of the runway." They circled half-a-dozen more times until they could get a bearing on our runway and lock it into their GPS. They were not sure if they could land with such poor visibility but they promised to try. Our hopes rose and fell each time they circled. Then suddenly, off at the far end of the runway, a shadow appeared out of the fog and in a whirl of snow the plane set down and roared up to our front door! It was such an emotional moment. We were dancing about like silly kids, hugging each other and dashing about sharing our happiness. The side door opened and out popped four women in bright red suits, plus Geoff and Nobby.

It was great to see Geoff. I wished we could have sat down in a pub with a couple of beers and had a heart-to-heart talk. I had so many questions to ask about the dynamics back at Base, what was happening between First Air and the Polar Relay expedition, what stories did the Alpha Team relate of their experience…. There was no time since changeover happened so fast. As Denise and I changed out of our dirty trail clothes, sorted through our personal resupply boxes and picked up our mail, Geoff gave us an update on our new team members and went over the re-supply list. "Yes, the Berwin bindings are on," he informed us. Thanks to Geoff for putting in a late night to mount them with new screw inserts to prevent the screws from pulling out. Nobby personally gave me the requested box of Tampax. He said, "I hope you appreciate what I had to go through to get these." Nobby related his story. Inexperienced in buying Tampax, he took a couple of turns past the store shelf where women's items such Tampax were kept. He was perplexed. Should he buy small, medium or large? It was some time before he got up the courage to ask the women at the checkout counter for assistance, "What size of Tampax should I buy for a woman about 5'4," 130 lbs.?" What a brave man! "Thanks, Nobby, I'll be thinking of you on the trail," I assured him.

Time was moving so fast with so many details to attend to. Compared to our simple life of the last two weeks, changeovers are a shock to my system. I felt so rushed saying good-bye to Rose, Karen, Catherine and Emma. At 5:00 a.m. the plane took off, taking our Bravo friends south.

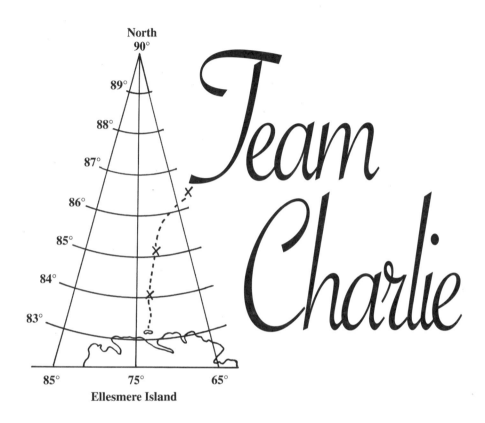

**North
90°**

89°
88°
87°
86°
85°
84°
83°

85° 75° 65°

Ellesmere Island

*Team
Charlie*

Day 30 Charlie Day 1

APRIL 12, 1997

A.M. latitude N 85° 09.978' longitude W 74° 16.525'
P.M. latitude N 85° 16.852' longitude W 73° 24.148'
Distance traveled: 5 nm Total nm from Ward Hunt: 131 nm
Hours traveled: 7 hrs. Total nm to North Pole: 285 nm
Total hours traveled: 168.5 hrs. Temperature: P.M. -24° C

After the snow settled from the departing Twin Otter, Denise and I called the new Charlie relay team together. It was 5:00 a.m. None of us had had much sleep, so we set up the tent, had hot drinks and slept till 12:30 p.m.

We were up and moving north by 3:00 p.m., putting in a good seven-hour day. It felt like a long day, with heavy pulks. On this third leg of the relay, we are hauling 60 liters of fuel plus 17 days of food, including three emergency days. I find it disheartening to be pulling a heavy pulk again.

We were lucky today; we did not encounter any leads, just endless hours of snow dunes, small pans and one- to two-meter high pressure ridges. Who said that it gets flatter after 120 nautical miles out from Ward Hunt Island?!! I felt very disoriented navigating today. For 29 days we have started at 9:00 a.m. with the sun on my left (west) shoulder; today, or rather this evening, the sun was on my right (east) shoulder.

Denise and I watched this new group to assess their strengths and weaknesses: to ascertain who had difficulty skiing their pulks up and over hummocks and who was able to haul their pulks hand-over-hand up steep pitches. Already we've noticed that Sue and Victoria Riches (mother and daughter) are the stronger participants.

Sue is a tall, elegant woman. At age 50 she takes the ice and snow obstacles in stride, even though this is her first outdoor adventure. From Sue I feel a deep sense of appreciation for life; she has recently recovered from breast cancer surgery. Sue lives with her husband in the West Midlands, at Small Place, which I imagine to be a small English country estate with climbing roses and carriage barns around back. Now that her three children are off on their own, she paints, runs a catering company, and is instrumental in organizing the World Driving (horses, that is) Championships for the Disabled.

Victoria, or Vic, but NOT Vicki, is 26—that age at which everything is possible if you want it badly enough. Vic is a tall woman like her mother and has an invincible attitude. She and her Mom are best of chums, but Vic often slips into an exasperated daughter/mother tone of "Oh, Mother, how could you be so forgetful!" Is my own daughter, Sarah, going to talk to me like this one day?

The other two Charlie Team members are Paula Power and Lynne Clarke. Both are small women, each under 50 kilograms. Today I could see that they were having difficulty hauling their heavy pulks over mounds of snow and ice. I have not gotten to know them well yet, as they are both quiet and don't give their opinions unless asked. Paula is single and works in information technology for a multi-national chemicals company. Lynne works as a quantity surveyor. She and her husband are recently back from Australia with their two small children.

We made camp at 10:00 p.m. and plan to be in bed by 12:30 a.m. It will take a couple of days to roll our days back to "normal."

――――――――――――――― *Day 31 Charlie Day 2* ―――――――――――――――

APRIL 13, 1997

A.M.	latitude N 85° 17.491'	longitude W 73° 08.297'	
P.M.	latitude N 85° 23.763'	longitude W 73° 25.411'	
Distance traveled: 7 nm		Total nm from Ward Hunt: 138 nm	
Hours traveled: 7.5 hrs.		Total nm to North Pole: 278 nm	
Total hours traveled: 176 hrs.		Temperature: P.M. -24° C	

Another long day. More snow dunes, ice pans, pressure ridges and cracks of small to medium size. The only memorable event of the day was when Denise attempted to jump a wide crack. When she landed, the far bank crumbled, leaving her precariously balanced with one foot dangling in the water. Before I could cross to assist her, she had pulled herself out.

Eric, my son, I was thinking about you and your Winnie-the-Pooh buddies. When I am leading, challenged by navigating and route finding, I am Tigger, with lots of "Bounce, Bounce, Bounce." When I am plodding along in the middle, watching my skis, I am Pooh Bear, "Ho Hum, Tiddly Pom." When I am dragging along at the back of the line, I am Eeyore, feeling very sorry for myself, "Oh, poor me, I hurt all over, my pulk is too heavy; no one cares to come back and help me when I get stuck...."

Already individual travel preferences have emerged. None in this relay team are keen to take on navigation and leading responsibilities. "You lead, we are happy to follow." Paula and Lynne prefer to be behind Denise or me when we are leading, as they find it too depressing and feel left behind when they travel at the end of the line. Sue and Vic, on the other hand, don't mind being at the back where they can stop to chat and make clothing adjustments without holding up traffic. They help each other and with their long strides they can easily catch up.

Day 32 Charlie Day 3

APRIL 14, 1997

A.M. *latitude N 85° 24.009'*   *longitude W 73° 24.014'*
P.M. *latitude N 85° 30.654'*   *longitude W 73° 37.498'*
Distance traveled: 7 nm   *Total nm from Ward Hunt: 145 nm*
Hours traveled: 8 hrs.   *Total nm to North Pole: 271 nm*
Total hours traveled: 184 hrs.   *Temperature: P.M. -30° C*

"Rise and Shine" at 7:30 a.m. On the trail from 10:00 a.m. to 6:00 p.m. We had a slight change in the terrain today. There were longer stretches of flat pans followed by "a mess-of-shit," to quote Denise.

There is something magical and mysterious about the ice on newly frozen leads. Earlier in the expedition when the temperatures were colder, the ice crystals grew on the new sea ice like chrysanthemum flowers or feathers. Now, the new ice on frozen leads is covered with snow crystals, similar to a thick carpet of fuzz. It reminds me of looking down from a plane onto a forest of deciduous trees.

chrysanthemum   feathers   fuzz-balls   bottle-brush

These fuzzy snow crystals contributed to a hard day; it was extremely difficult to ski and drag our pulks on this carpet of fuzz. My thigh muscles burned, the sweat poured down my back and I had to lean so hard into my harness that it was hard to breathe. In previous weeks, we went out of our way to travel on the newly frozen leads, as they offered highways of flat and smooth gliding. Today it was such hard work that we were glad to get off them. I wonder what makes this snow different. Could it be the salt content in the snow crystals?

On one newly frozen lead we stopped to take photos of the beautiful ice sculptures created by the elastic properties of the young sea ice. While the ice was still a flexible ten centimeters thin, pressure squeezed the new ice, causing layers to ride over each other and rise to heights of one meter. These ice slabs gracefully bent and curled like dried leaves before freezing solid in the cold polar air.

We traveled eight hours and gained seven nautical miles. Yesterday we only made five nautical miles. Team Charlie is discouraged by their lack of progress. They arrived on the ice with a goal of gaining two degrees north (120 nautical miles). This means that they must average nine nautical miles a day. On my schedule I have Team Charlie on the ice for 13 full travel days, averaging 7 nautical miles a day, for a total of 91 nautical miles. I fear that they have set an unrealistic goal.

I am starting to observe a pattern. Each team arrives on the ice with an attitude of "let's knock off those miles" and "we can conquer the Arctic with brute force and British determination." I agree it is important to set goals but I am a firm believer that the goals must be achievable. It is much better to be realistic or even conservative with mileage in the arctic regions, given the variable factors of weather and ice conditions. It is better for team morale to be ahead of schedule rather than behind.

It is hard for me to explain my intuitive feeling that we cannot force the Arctic to yield miles with bull-headed strength. We can only go as far and as fast as she lets us. We must use our intuition to feel her moods. Travel long and hard when the weather is good and rest when the weather is bad. I have also sensed these feelings climbing in the mountains of Peru and Bolivia. Because I respected the mountains, I was allowed to climb to their lofty peaks.

I saw fresh fox tracks again, 145 nautical miles from land! A reminder to scan the horizon for polar bears when we crawl out of the tent in the morning, before we squat behind the ice to answer the call of nature, and to look behind us when we ski through the rough ice.

On the sched call this evening, Michael told Denise that her friend Magnus has passed away. Magnus had been Denise's partner for many years. Magnus also worked for the Canadian Outward Bound Wilderness School, so I knew him well. He was suffering from a long terminal illness. Denise is taking it hard.

Day 33 Charlie Day 4

APRIL 15, 1997

A.M. latitude N 85° 30.549'	longitude W 73° 38.935'
P.M. latitude N 85° 36.703'	longitude W 73° 52.319'
Distance traveled: 6 nm	Total nm from Ward Hunt: 151 nm
Hours traveled: 8 hrs.	Total nm to North Pole: 265 nm
Total hours traveled: 192 hrs.	Temperature: P.M. -25° C

Up at 6:00 a.m. We reorganized our pulk weights and got off by 9:30 a.m. It was a dreary overcast day—windy, with flat light and poor visibility. After a hard two hours of hauling over soft snow dunes, we hit some old large leads that, miracle of miracles, stretched due north! What luck. The ice seems to have changed. Leads and pressure ridges now run due north. The landscape—or rather icescape—looks flatter. I shouldn't speak too soon; it may be a short-lived illusion.

After eight hours of good travel on leads and snow highways, it was hard to believe the GPS indicated only six nautical miles north. How discouraging, most of us had bet on at least eight miles. It is difficult for me to comprehend how we can be working so hard, for so many hours, and yet gain so few miles. Our bodies complain that they are working overtime. It's always push, push, push, and yet we seem to be on a treadmill going nowhere. Is this another Sedna joke?

Paula did not eat her breakfast this morning. She said she doesn't like the Hot Crunchy cereal. She and Lynne are hauling the fuel, which gives them the lightest pulks. Within the first hour, Paula was dragging. Lynne confided to me that Paula had told her that morning, "I'm not up for it today." Denise took some of Paula's weight but still she lagged. When we hit a big old lead, I decided to test a hunch. (The Tigger test.) I asked Paula to go ahead and break trail across the lead. She took off, at a fast pace that was hard for the rest of us to match. This confirmed my guess that it was her attitude that was dragging her down, not her physical weakness. It's not that Paula has a bad attitude; but instead I think she is overwhelmed by the Arctic and this is affecting her physical output. While setting up camp, Paula, having pulled a light pulk all day, was full of energy. There were a few mumbles like, "Maybe you should pull my pulk tomorrow." I worry that her attitude may jeopardize the collective strength of the group. How will she deal with situations if conditions get worse? Will she find deeper inner strengths or emotionally give up? From my experience leading Outward Bound groups, I have seen a physically weaker person, when faced with an insurmountable challenge, find enormous inner strength while another stronger person falls apart. According to her teammates, Paula was one of the strongest on the selection weekends.

I led all day as Denise was not up for leading. She skied at the back of the group and didn't participate much in conversations during breaks. She wants some time alone to deal with Magnus' death.

Shit, I'm getting rained on inside the tent. It's so warm in the tent tonight that the frost is melting on the inner tent liner, dripping into my journal as I write! A sure sign that outside temperatures are warming up.

Day 34 Charlie Day 5

APRIL 16, 1997

A.M.	*latitude N 85° 38.486'*	*longitude W 73° 40.715'*
P.M.	*latitude N 85° 45.122'*	*longitude W 73° 46.254'*
Distance traveled: 9 nm		*Total nm from Ward Hunt: 160 nm*
Hours traveled: 9 hrs.		*Total nm to North Pole: 256 nm*
Total hours traveled: 201 hrs.		*Temperature: P.M. -22° C*

We skied nine hours and gained nine nautical miles north! A record for Team Charlie. The team morale is on a high. They are calculating how many nautical miles they need to increase their daily mileage by in order to meet their goal of 120 nautical miles.

While climbing over a pressure ridge this morning, I had the most amazing taste sensation of freshly squeezed oranges. It was, wow! I've never experienced such a strong smell/taste sensation. Maybe my nose is tired of smelling the nothing of snow and my brain executed a rerun.

I led again all day. Denise was still feeling depressed about Magnus. Her preference was to pull a heavier pulk and bring up the rear-end. We talked in the tent tonight about how hard it is to let go of someone you love, how lucky she was to have spent a week with him before coming north and how Magnus had suffered from his illness and was now at peace from the pain he bore for so many years. The tears ran down her face and I reached over and gave her a hug.

Day 35 Charlie Day 6

APRIL 17, 1997

A.M.	*latitude N 85° 45.437'*	*longitude W 73° 42.320'*
P.M.	*latitude N 85° 54.233'*	*longitude W 73° 51.789'*
Distance traveled: 9 nm		*Total nm from Ward Hunt: 169 nm*
Hours traveled: 8.5 hrs.		*Total nm to North Pole: 247 nm*
Total hours traveled: 209.5 hrs.		*Temperature: P.M. -25° C*

We skied for 8.5 hours and covered nine nautical miles for the second day in a row. This is better. We are starting to show some progress for our efforts. I say it softly for fear that Sedna will throw more challenges at us.

For the last two days, the ice has resembled a moonscape, with the large ice pans looking like craters surrounded by pointed mountains of ice blocks. It reminds me of a science set that I was given for Christmas when I was ten or eleven years old. Into a glass sphere of water I sprinkled crystals. After a couple of days, the crystals grew into a moonscape of pastel colors. I wonder if they still sell that set; Sarah and Eric would enjoy having one.

This evening in the Captain's Log I recorded the following under team morale: Victoria had a "not so good day." Paula was "knackered" when we arrived at camp. Lynne said that "the first two hours were bad, the rest of the day okay, and the last hour dragged on." Sue had a "nine" day (on a scale of one to ten, ten being the highest). Denise was "up after two days of being down." And I "need more sleep." I find it interesting how Paula, young and strong, was "knackered," while the older Sue, pulling a heavier pulk had a "9" day. I wonder if they are evaluating the day from similar scales or points of view. Perhaps Sue had just as hard a day as Paula, but—interpreted from her life experience—it did not pull her down. I hope than when I am 50, I can move as gracefully through the hardships of life as Sue.

I have not slept well the last two nights. I'm too hot. Even stripped down to my capeline under-wear and with the top layer of the Stephenson sleeping bag unzipped, I wake up wet with the inside of my VBL dripping. I don't understand. It's -24° C. I have slept in more clothes in the summer and never have been so wet! Why is this happening? Is it a reaction to going to bed right after eating? Am I having hot flashes? Or am I acclimatizing so well to the cold that -24° C is too hot? Tonight I will commit the sin of not sleeping in my VBL to see if I can improve my sleep.

I am discreetly nibbling on maple sugar candy that Mom sent in with the last resupply. Yummy. Thanks for your support, Mom. It means a lot to me out here...on this lonely planet of ice. Today's theme song was, "I'm so tired, my mind is on the blink, I'm so tired, I haven't slept a wink..."

Day 36 Charlie Day 7

APRIL 18, 1997

A.M.	*latitude N 85° 55.030'*	*longitude W 73° 37.914'*	
P.M.	*latitude N 86° 02.269'*	*longitude W 73° 42.601'*	
Distance traveled: 8 nm		*Total nm from Ward Hunt: 177 nm*	
Hours traveled: 8.5 hrs.		*Total nm to North Pole: 239 nm*	
Total hours traveled: 218 hrs.		*Temperature: P.M. -27° C*	

Last night we drifted almost .8 of a minute of latitude north and 13 minutes of longitude east. This translates to .8 nautical miles north and .8 nautical miles east. (Lines of latitude are equal distances apart; therefore one degree always equals 60 nautical miles. Whereas the lines of longitude are not parallel and become closer together as you near the North Pole. At our present location, 13 minutes equals .8 nautical miles.) Every day we have pushed north-northwest and still we are on the 73rd meridian. I'd like to get back to the 74th.

We traveled for 8.5 hours and gained eight nautical miles north. My feet are throbbing. The rest of the group is feeling the miles too. For Paula, who is 5'2" with a slight build, "the first seven hours were okay, after that it was the pits." Vic had an "okay day, but not brilliant." Lynne "enjoyed the day except the last 1 1/2 hours killed me off." Sue, chipper as always, said that she was "often in a trance; I had a nice day, but lost my oomph."

I'm starting to feel rundown too. I've developed a deep cough; if I don't get more sleep and get myself back up, I'm afraid this cough will settle down into my lungs and put me out of the running. Denise and I have been on the trail for 36 days—without any time off from the groups. This is the longest that I have been continuously on the trail. On the Baffin Island Expedition, (the 4,000 kilometer dog-sledding journey around Baffin Island that I did with Paul), four weeks was the longest time that we were on the trail between communities. At each community we had the opportunity to shower, phone my mother and talk to Sarah and Eric, gorge on fresh fruit and vegetables, wash clothes and sleep in a warm bed, before pushing on to the next community.

Even though we are all physically sore and tired, mentally and emotionally we are happy to have inched across the 86th degree of latitude.

Day 37 Charlie Day 8

APRIL 19, 1997

A.M.	latitude N 86° 02.272'	longitude W 73° 05.007'
P.M.	latitude N 86° 06.717'	longitude W 72° 22.387'
Distance traveled: 5 nm		Total nm from Ward Hunt: 182 nm
Hours traveled: 6 hrs.		Total nm to North Pole: 234 nm
Total hours traveled: 224 hrs.		Temperature: P.M. -22° C

Today we found ourselves in an endless maze of pressure ice and small leads. The snow between the pressure ridges was deep, soft and a killer on the lower back to pull through. Today was one of the few days that I was glad we didn't have to get a dog team through this chaos. Our day consisted of the following routine. We skied to a pressure ridge and took our skis off and either lashed them onto our pulk or threw them over the pressure ridge. We scrambled over the slippery ice chunks, careful not to smash our shins. At the top of the ridge, we pulled and yanked our pulk up. When the pulk misbehaved and refused to follow, we climbed back down to free it or flip it back

March 14, 1997, we made a final check of pulks before departing Ward Hunt Island, off the northern tip of Ellesmere Island. From here it is 416 nautical miles to the North Pole.

When the ice-pack, pressed south by polar ocean currents, meets the land mass of Ellesmere Island, it is heaved up into a massive jumble of ice.

Rest stops for a glug of water, a handful of snacks, and a quick pee were short,
as cool-down time was very rapid.

Teamwork was often required to lift and shove the heavy pulks up and over pressure ridges.

Denise leading the group through ice rubble.

Day 7, breaking camp on the shores of The Big Lead. Luck was with us:
the lead had frozen over during the night.

Refrozen leads offered highways through the pressure ice, but rarely did they head north.

The challenges of route-finding involved navigating the most direct line northward, while avoiding high pressure ridges and wide open leads.

Team Alfa (from left): Ann Daniels, Jan McCormac, Sue Fullilove, and Clair Fletcher.

For me, leading these "ordinary British women" on a journey
across the polar ice was an amazing experience.

I was fascinated by the variety and beauty of the ice crystals that formed on new ice.

Victoria Riches (Sue's daughter),
an invincible age 23.

Sue Riches, age 50, takes life's
challenges in stride.

Sue and Victoria sitting on ice floaters moments after their swim.

Denise Martin, my assistant leader, who returned for a second swim to rescue vital equipment.

Denise making a desperate swim for the far shore.

Sue and Victoria stranded on floating chunks of ice as the lead continued to open. On the far shore, Denise is pulled up the bank by Paula and Lynn.

Approximately every two weeks, the plane brought in the next relay team of four and lifted out the returning team.

Team Charlie (from left to right): Paula, Victoria, Denise (with penguin), Sue, Lynn and Matty.

Crossing leads offered problem-solving challenges and adrenaline rushes.

Stepping over thin ice.

Skiing in ground storm conditions was exhilarating for the first day;
by the second and third day it became tedious.

On overcast days, navigation was difficult. There were no shadows to orient direction and, with poor visibility, compass bearings had to be taken often.

As we neared the North Pole, the ice became less heaved by pressure ridges but more fractured, necessitating numerous detours around open leads.

Matty and Denise at the Geographic North Pole.

With my family (from left): Matty, Sarah, Paul, and Eric.

upright. We descended the ridge and ran for our life to make sure the pulk did not run us over. No time to rest; it was back to help the others. When everyone was over, we strapped our skis on, skied for another three to five minutes over cracks and small leads until another pressure ridge loomed into sight. We repeated the above scenario.

It seemed futile to waste time putting and taking off our skis for such a short duration between the pressure ridges. We tried walking without skis but the snow was too deep. Some of the ridges were not too difficult to ski over but our bindings could not take the side torquing stress. Charlie Team brought in skis mounted with a hybrid binding consisting of the borrowed Berwin toe pieces and the Uni-Flex base plate and heel system. This seemed like a good solution, as the Berwin base plates are known to snap, and we have broken many Uni-Flex toe bails. However, two days ago, Sue snapped the plastic Uni-Flex base plate on her binding. Today Paula's plastic base is starting to crack. This is not good! This time I am prepared; at the changeover I picked up four spare bindings, plus additional parts.

The high point for me this afternoon was photographing the team traveling over snow dunes in a ground storm. (A ground storm is caused by the wind whipping up loose snow, not from snow descending from the heavens.) Often there were clear blue skies overhead, while a white-out blizzard raged around our legs. The moving snow blurred the harsh lines of ice forms. The team was an undulating line of backlit forms emerging from soft brilliant light. The back of the line faded into shadows as the front of the line came into color. Eerie, yet extremely beautiful.

I recognize that when I don't take out my camera it is because I am either bored or stressed out with the responsibility of leading, the physical work or the cold.

My low for the day is the fact that we are drifting east at an alarming rate. Since setting up camp, we have moved from: 72° 22.387' at 5:00 p.m. to 72° 05.851' at 8:00 p.m. This equals 16.536 minutes to the east or just over one nautical mile in three hours. This easterly drift worries me. Both Will Steger and Richard Weber have stressed the importance of staying close to the 74th line of longitude. On the ocean floor, along this longitude line, runs the Lomonosov Ridge. This ridge influences the ocean currents. East of the 74th the ocean currents become increasingly stronger. If we get caught too far east, we may be pulled into a polar drift that will carry us east and southeast faster than we can ski north and northwest. If that happens, this expedition will fail to reach the North Pole.

We saw fox tracks again today, 182 miles from Ward Hunt Island.

Day 38 Charlie Day 9

APRIL 20, 1997

A.M.	latitude N 86° 06.067'	longitude W 69° 46.188'
P.M.	latitude N 86° 06.970'	longitude W 68° 42.893'
Distance traveled: 0 nm		Total nm from Ward Hunt: 182 nm

Hours traveled: 0 hrs.   *Total nm to North Pole: 234 nm*
Total hours traveled: 224 hrs.   *Temperature: P.M. -20° C*

I woke up to the sound of the tent walls flapping in the wind. From the warm depths of my sleeping bag it sounded nasty. I could hear the sounds of crushing ice moving to the south. (Interesting: even from my sleeping bag I knew which direction was south.) But from the comfort of my sleeping bag was not a reliable way to evaluate the weather. Before giving the "Rise and Shine" call, I headed out for a pee and walk-about. The wind was not bad around the tent situated in the lea of the ice ridge. I clambered up the ridge to get a reading on the wind speed. It was gusting so hard that I could lie back in the arms of the wind and feel the wind pummeling me with soft punches. With my back to the wind it was not brutally cold, but when I faced into the wind, my face was sandblasted with blowing snow. No doubt about it, this was stormy weather. When I got back in the tent, I gave my weather report, "Winds are from the southwest, gusting 40–80 kph, visibility is 100 meters at best, temperature -23° C. It's a good day to lay over." My announcement was welcomed with a muffled cheer from a row of lumpy sleeping bags. I snuggled back into my still-warm sleeping bag to finish off a good dream.

We all slept till 11:45 a.m.! What a luxury. This was followed by a "delicious" breakfast of Hot Crunchy (for the 38th day in a row), coffee, which stimulated a trip out to "walk the turtle" and be energized by the wind. Then back into the tent to eat and drink more. I wrote a letter to Sarah to wish her a happy birthday and to Eric to ask about his time with his grandmother in Northern Ontario.

I worked on domestic chores. I replaced the Velcro on the warm-up pants that Greg (a good friend and NorthWinds' base manager during my absence) lent me. Now I have the option of skiing without them falling down around my ankles. The wind is still beating on the tent. The center ski holding the tent up is bent to the extreme. I hope it doesn't break—it is my ski! It's even windy inside the tent. I'm not sure if the wind is coming through the thin nylon tent walls or if the inside currents are caused by the tent walls flapping in and out. The steam rising from my mug of hot chocolate wafts, right, left, right, left....

Victoria has been asked to take responsibility for tape recording our experiences of living on the ice. She has not had the time or energy during the last couple of days and asked us to refresh her memory. Then she calls for "Silence" and in her delightful British accent, rambles on about our little adventures. This afternoon she has been doing interviews. "Paula, what has it been like for you..." Paula responds, "It has been hard and amazing...." Next to be interviewed is Lynne. "Lynne, is this experience what you expected?" Lynne, "No, but then I really did not know what to expect...."

Melting snow for hot drinks, eating, writing, reading and worrying about our easterly drift filled out our agenda for the day. I hope this storm blows over so we can travel tomorrow.

Day 39 Charlie Day 10

APRIL 21, 1997

A.M.   latitude N 86° 07.779'   longitude W 67° 44.105'
P.M.   latitude N 86° 10.200'   longitude W 67° 59.200'
Distance traveled: 3 nm   Total nm from Ward Hunt: 185 nm
Hours traveled: 6 hrs.   Total nm to North Pole: 231 nm
Total hours traveled: 230 hrs.   Temperature: P.M. -19° C

"Rise and Shine" at 6:00 a.m. The good news this morning was that the sun had warmed our planet up to –19 C° and the winds had decreased to 25–35 kph. It was still a nasty morning but not enough to prevent us from traveling. Upon checking our GPS during breakfast, we discovered we are now at W 67° 44.105'. This was bad news; since we stopped traveling on the afternoon of April 19, we have drifted from 72° 22.387' to 67° 44.105', a drift of 4° 38.282'. At our present location of 86° N, one degree of longitude equals four nautical miles—therefore our total drift was 19.676 nautical miles EAST!! We must be over the top of Greenland by now.

Just after we finished packing up, it started to snow, our visibility decreased and the light flattened. Denise made the unusual comment that, "This feels like a weird day." Little did either of us know that disaster would befall us before its end.

Because of the radical easterly drift, I decided to push west. Morale was low. Charlie Team had to face the fact that they would not be able to reach their goal of 120 nautical miles north. To save the expedition, they needed to sacrifice the glory of their own goal and, instead, push the route back to the 74th meridian. The gray day matched our gray mood and our hearts dragged as we skied on. Even our snack breaks allowed us minimal relief from the constant wind and blowing snow.

Yesterday powerful winds scoured the ice and deposited deep drifts of soft snow in the pressure ridges. As we lumbered over the ridges, we stepped into cracks camouflaged by snow, bruising our shins and twisting our knees. Between the ridges, the snow was so hard packed that our pulks side-slipped off bumps, pulling us off balance.

At 2:30 p.m., shortly after our third break, we came to an open lead of black water, running north- south. Since we were traveling in a westerly direction, we had to cross this lead. I found a section choked with frozen ice. My gut feeling was, "I don't like this…" but my head rationalized the situation, "we've been over worse ice than this." As I crossed, I stopped often to test the ice with my ski pole. Most of the ice consisted of hard slippery chunks; however, there were a few soft slushy spots where I could thrust my ski pole through. I was concerned that the women might fall on the slippery ice and punch through a slush hole. Not seeing a better option, I continued, calling back, "follow my tracks." When I reached the far bank, I removed my skis to enable me to jump a small crack onto the high bank. I scrambled up the bank and pulled my pulk up and out of the way. Not a minute later when I returned to help Denise get up the bank, I noticed that the small crack had increased to one meter wide. I suggested to Denise that she lead the team north around the crack and climb on the bank over there. I stood and watched Denise lead off with Sue and Victoria not far behind. Lynne and Paula were some distance behind, just stepping onto the lead.

To my horror I saw Sue slowly begin to sink. I called out, "Sue, ski faster: you are sinking!" She stopped to look down, and sure enough, the heels of her skis were sinking. Before she had time to move forward she slipped backwards, lost her balance and sank chest-deep into slushy ice water. When I yelled, Denise looked back. Seeing Sue in the water she quickly unclipped from her pulk, and in a calm voice assured Sue, "It's okay Sue, we'll get you out, just hang on." Denise circled around Sue to get a hold of the rope that attached Sue to her pulk. Victoria unclipped from her pulk and went to assist Denise. "It's okay, Mother, we'll get you out." Pulling together, Victoria and Denise managed to haul Sue up on an ice chunk. As I watched, stranded on the far shoreline, I noticed the ice in the lead was quickly and silently shifting apart. Five minutes ago the bridge of frozen ice chunks that I had traveled across had been an opaque gray-blue; now black cracks were growing between the ice blocks. Oh, shit! I called out to Denise, Sue and Victoria, " The lead is breaking up! Head back to the far bank, fast!"

I ran to my pulk to retrieve the throw-line rescue bag and threw it out to Denise, thinking that she would need it to assist Victoria and Sue back to the far shore. Helpless from the west bank, I yelled, "It's breaking up: get off the lead!" Victoria hesitated; she wanted to make sure that her Mom was okay. As the lead continued to open, the pressure holding the ice blocks together released and the bridge disintegrated. Sue sank again into the slushy ice. Denise and Victoria struggled to pull her up on a larger ice chunk. Suddenly all three were sinking, grappling to find solid ice, their skis dragging them down.

My worst nightmare was unfolding before me!

I yelled to Lynne and Paula, who could not see what was happening. "Get off the lead. Get off the lead! It's breaking up! Move fast, we need your help!" I waved my arms to indicate for them to move up the far bank opposite me. Powerless to help, I watched Denise struggle towards the east bank. Each time she hauled herself out of the water, the ice gave way and sank under her weight. She fought through the icy slush, pulling up, sinking again and again. My heart rose and sank with her. It was awful to watch. I called again to Paula and Lynne, who were still unaware of the disaster that was unfolding, "Lynne, Paula, hurry! Help Denise, she is in the water! Hurry!"

Ten meters from me, Sue managed to pull herself up on a small floater, barely large enough to support her weight. She had lost one boot, both skis and poles, but was still attached to her pulk which floated beside her in the now open lead. She sat tensely, not daring to move, with her thin-socked foot shivering. Two meters away Victoria struggled to pull herself up on a larger floater. She had lost her pulk, both skis and one pole. Each was more concerned for the other than herself. "Mom, it's going to be okay." "I'm okay, Victoria, I'm just worried about you." "What would Father say if he could see us now?" "I'm afraid that this is what he feared most." "Are you sure that you are okay, Mother?" "Yes, I'm okay, my foot is cold. Are you cold, dear?" "Mother, throw me your pulk rope, I'll pull you over."

Not being directly involved with the rescue, I was in a better position to keep a perspective on the big picture. All too often, when there is a crisis situation, everyone focuses on the initial accident oblivious to their own danger, and the situation snowballs into a more major crisis.

From my vantage point I could see Lynne and Paula on the far bank just staring at Denise, who was struggling through the ice and water. I hollered, "Hurry! Help pull her out!" Denise, with concentrated tenacity, half swimming, half crawling, dragged herself over the breaking ice. It seemed like an eternity before she managed to reach the far shore. Paula and Lynne reached out to pull her up the bank. I sighed with relief. One out, two to go.

The black waters continued to open around Sue and Victoria. They had managed to pull their floating ice islands together. My throw-line bag sat on the ice where a few moments before Denise had stood. In less than 10 minutes the far shore had moved 50 meters away. I now realized that I would need to pull Sue and Victoria to my shoreline. Think! Think! Think! At the bottom of my pulk was a five meter length of spare polypropylene rope. I dug it out and looped my ski poles together, attached the spare rope along with my pulk trace and swung it out to Victoria. It just reached her. With one arm Victoria held the rope and with the other, she extended her remaining ski pole to her mother. I pulled, Victoria braced herself, and ever so slowly the flotillas slid towards me. Victoria was getting stretched; there was too much pull on her arms. Sue had to move onto Victoria's larger ice block. Precariously balancing herself and numb with cold, she managed to make the shift without tipping off her wobbly floater. I dug my heels into the snow and, with Sue and Victoria both holding on, I managed to pull them towards me. 1 1/2 meters from the bank, their floater was halted by small slushy chunks of ice. Shit! Now what. Think! Think! Think! Sue's pulk, still attached to her, was floating behind her. I had her pull the pulk around to bridge the gap and instructed them to use the pulk as a stepping stone to leap up on the bank. Sue went first, Victoria followed. What a relief to have everyone on solid ice.

Sue was shivering with cold and very concerned about her freezing foot. My first priority was not Sue's foot, but to keep Sue and Victoria's core temperature from dropping. Our situation was ominous. Our only shelter from the harsh arctic environment was the tent in Denise's pulk which was out floating on the open lead. I took Sue behind an ice hummock out of the wind. While I pulled out my down parka and took off my warm-up pants for Sue, Victoria rummaged through Sue's pulk to pull out Sue's parka and warm-up pants which she put on. Once Sue and Victoria were bundled up and out of the wind, I removed the sock from Sue's shivering foot. Good, no white toes, just a very pink and blue foot. Sue put her bare foot on my bare chest. Wow was that cold! When my chest cooled off, she tucked her toes in one arm pit, then the other. Sue confessed that after her foot was "saved" she felt "much better." Next problem was that Sue had only one boot. I dug out a spare pair of boot liners from my pulk and emptied a stuff sac to pull over the liners. It would have to do for now, as my boots were too small for either Sue or Victoria.

While attending to Sue and Victoria, I was keeping an eye on the far side. Denise was heading back out on the fractured ice to rescue equipment. Brave woman! Tied to a makeshift rope of pulk traces, she was belayed (attached to a safety rope) by Paula and Lynne. Denise first retrieved Victoria's pulk and skis, as they were on firmer ice. She then skied cautiously back to her pulk, which carried the essential tent and radio. Denise attached the pulk trace to her and started back towards the far shore. Suddenly the ice gave way and Denise plunged into the freezing ocean once more. Paula and Lynne, with feet braced, strained to haul Denise and her pulk through the breaking ice. Denise, exhausted from her first swim and the cold rapidly draining her strength, struggled through the ice chunks. But the weight of her saturated clothes was dragging her down. Denise was unable to keep her skis on the surface and in a desperate struggle, she kicked off her boots, losing both skis and boots. After what seemed like an endless space of time, Paula and Lynne dragged Denise up the bank. She stood exhausted, dripping wet in her stocking feet. My heart was full of pride that Denise had braved a second swim to rescue the tent and radio. I also feared that she would drop quickly into a hypothermic state. The far shore continued to slip further away and we now had to shout to communicate. To add to our precarious situation, it began to snow lightly, decreasing visibility. From the far bank it was impossible for me to accurately assess Denise's deteriorating condition. I knew she was seriously losing to the cold when she was unable to give Paula and Lynn instructions and started yelling, "Matty, my fucking feet are freezing!"

Fearing that Denise would soon be unable to help herself, I hollered back, "Lynne, Paula, set up the tent. Get Denise out of her wet clothes, into a sleeping bag and into dry clothes!"

Denise kept yelling "My FUCKING feet are freezing!!!!"

"Denise," I yelled back, "use a pair of Lynne and Paula's boot liners." (Our boots each had double insulated liners that could be pulled apart.) "Paula, Lynne, you need to move fast: Denise's condition is serious." Paula and Lynne moved into action and started setting the tent up.

We were in a crisis situation. We were separated by a 50-meter-wide lead that was open as far north and south as I could see. Denise, Paula, and Lynne had the tent and radio. Sue, Victoria and I had the pots and stoves. Three women had had a plunge in the cold Arctic Ocean and were bordering on hypothermia. We had lost boots, skis and poles. On the far shore, I had two clients, with no previous winter or arctic experience, caring for Denise, my assistant leader and dear friend. (Or, at this moment in time, my closest friend.)

I checked on Sue and Victoria who were sheltered behind an ice chunk, eating and drinking. They were fine. I heard Lynne yelling to me. She told me that Denise was in the tent in a sleeping bag and warming up. I shouted that I would head north with Sue and Victoria to find a place to cross the lead. I had no idea if this would take 30 minutes or…I dreaded to imagine, more than a day. I explained that they too must head north along the lead as soon as Denise was able to travel.

Victoria, Sue and I headed north. We were a pathetic sight, three lone figures, stumbling alongside a foreboding black lead, dragging but two pulks. (Sue and Victoria insisted on pulling the pulks to help them rewarm.) On and on we went, encountering numerous secondary leads branching off the main lead. (This is a common occurrence, to have secondary leads cracking off perpendicular to the main lead.) I began to worry about the very real possibility that the others might also encounter secondary leads and be forced up a branching lead. The image of two groups wandering the sea ice as the visibility decreased and the winds blew over our tracks was not a pleasant one. I shared my thoughts with Sue and Victoria and suggested that if they were warm enough, we'd wait until we could see the others tromping up the opposite shore. They assured me that they were toasty warm. Visibility had decreased to a half-kilometer. I could see no chance to cross the ever-widening lead.

We needed a miracle.

As we waited, Sue noticed that the lead was closing. It happened so quickly. Within 20 seconds, the two shores crunched to within two meters of each other. The slushy ice between them became, under pressure, hard as cement. Quickly, we scrambled down one bank and hurried up the far one. Twenty minutes later we met Denise, Lynne and Paula just crossing a branching lead. I was so relieved to have the group reunited and to see that Denise, a little tired but back in form, was wresting pulks over ice obstacles and barking out directions to Lynne and Paula. We were now safe from the unforgiving arctic environment. My fears of spending an uncomfortable night (half without tent, half without stoves) receded.

The snow was letting up and the skies brightened. Dragging pulks loaded with the ice-encrusted gear that Denise had rescued and her pile of frozen clothes, we headed north till we found a "safe camping spot," a large unbroken pan. It was 4:30 p.m. After we erected the tent, our security talisman, our anxieties dissolved and we became euphoric with giddy laughter. All talked at once and hugged each other as if we were long-lost comrades.

Inside the tent, our hands cupped around our hot drinks, we tried to piece together exactly what had happened. Like the four blind men trying to describe an elephant, each of us had experienced the drama from a different angle. Lynne and Paula explained that they had not fully grasped the seriousness of the situation until they climbed over the bank and saw Sue and Victoria stranded on floaters and Denise struggling to swim towards them. At this point Paula informed us, "I got it all on video!" Sue and Victoria shared what it had been like to take a dip in the Arctic Ocean. "No, really," exclaimed Victoria, "I was so warm and had so many clothes on that I really did not feel the cold water. I wasn't worried about myself, I was worried about Mom. I knew that she would say that she was all right, even if she wasn't, so that I wouldn't worry." "Victoria," countered Sue, "Really, I was fine. I was concerned about my freezing foot and kept thinking about how upset your father would be." I turned to Denise, "Dam, you were brave to go back out there to risk a second swim!" Denise explained that before she got cold, she wanted to rescue as much equipment as possible. She had retrieved Victoria's pulk first as the ice was not deteriorating there and tossed abandoned skis and poles towards shore. Then she skied back to her pulk. "No way," Denise exclaimed, "was I going to leave my pulk out there with the tent, radio and my Nikon camera!" Paula and Lynne added that when Denise reached her pulk she had unclipped her safety rope and clipped it to her pulk. "Denise," they shouted, "stay clipped in, clip your pulk trace to you!" Moments after she clipped back onto the safely line, she went through again. Denise shared the somber truth, "If Lynne and Paula had not hauled me out, I doubt that I had the strength to have made the swim a second time."

After hot drinks and soup, I announced that we needed to attempt to retrieve as much lost equipment as possible, most importantly Denise's boots and skis. (Denise had rescued Sue's left boot.) While Victoria, Denise and Sue tended to their wet clothing, Paula, Lynne and I returned to the "scene of the crime." The scene had changed dramatically; the far shore where I had stood had slid further away and to the south. Everywhere the ice had fractured into islands. Not more than five meters from us we could see the tip of a ski, and beyond that poles protruding through the ice rubble. I was not particularly keen on risking a swim (although I did feel a twinge of guilt that I had not fallen in). The slushy ice rubble was not firm enough to support my weight, so we built a floating bridge of ice chunks that we dislodged from the bank. After 20 minutes our bridge had set up firmly enough for me to gingerly walk out, with Paula and Lynne keeping me belayed on a safety line. I was able to retrieve Denise's skis with boots still strapped in the bindings. Further out on the ice we left six poles and the throw-line-rescue bag. We returned to camp joyous with our good luck, dragging our wet trophies. If we could get the boots and outer clothing dry, we now had enough equipment to continue the expedition.

Knowing how easily communications over the radio can be misconstrued, I carefully wrote down exactly what we would communicate to Resolute on the evening's sched call. The information needed to be clear and simple so our message did not get confused. I read out what I would say to the women and rewrote words that might be misleading. After Denise filled in the "coms good," weather, location, etc., she handed me the microphone.

"We had an adventure. You need to record the following information."
Michael took a moment to set up the tape recorder, "Go ahead."
"Crossing a lead of frozen ice chunks, lead suddenly opened, splitting apart.
Three immersions: Denise, Sue and Victoria.
All now warm and happy.
Recovered all equipment, minus six ski poles."
"Roger, Roger," was Michael's down-to-business response.

Day 40 Charlie Day 11

APRIL 22, 1997

A.M. *latitude N 86° 09.668'*	*longitude W 67° 17.883'*
P.M. *latitude N 86° 12.339'*	*longitude W 67° 00.929'*
Distance traveled: 2 nm	*Total nm from Ward Hunt: 187 nm*
Hours traveled: 8 hrs.	*Total nm to North Pole: 229 nm*
Total hours traveled: 238 hrs.	*Temperature: P.M. -22° C*

Up at 6:00 a.m. There was a lot of clothing to dry, mostly boot liners and one-piece suits, before we could continue our northward crusade. Lynne, Denise and I returned to see if we could find and salvage any of the six missing ski poles. The lead had changed so much that, if our tracks had not led us to the spot, I would not have recognized it. Out on the refrozen lead, four ski poles were frozen in time as they reached out of their icy graves. It was eerie. We imagined how we would feel if we had come upon such a scene. It would have told a story where some or all were taken down to the bottom of the sea by Sedna.

Denise figured it was my turn to ski out on the thin ice. I suggested that she had more experience swimming with skis. She gave me a "not funny" look. "Okay, just joking!" I told her. I skied out while Lynne and Denise kept me on belay. I used the ice ax to chop out the throw-line bag and ski poles. I could see one more ski pole but it was not worth the risk to retrieve it. We decided to let Sedna keep it. A small sacrifice for our good luck.

It took us till 11:00 a.m. to get enough clothing and boot liners dried before we were able to break camp. For one kilometer we skied north along the "dreaded black lead" only to find that our progress was blocked by a branching lead. Interestingly, there was no trace of the bridge that had so miraculously formed yesterday for Sue, Vic and me. Vic sacrificed two Penguin bars to encourage Sedna to close the lead for us again. Sedna was not in the mood to make deals, so we turned east in hopes of finding a bridge. Much to our chagrin, this branching lead turned south. For a while, the women lingered at the bend, reluctant to retreat south. After one kilometer south we came to a possible crossing. I dropped down to test the ice. It was fine. I jumped hard on all the ice blocks and returned to retrieve my pulk. The group stood along the bank and watched; the scene reminded me of penguins peering into the ocean to see if the first penguin that fell in the water will be devoured by a leopard seal. Their confidence and nerves were shattered.

On the ice of the refrozen lead I noticed clumps of ice crystals the size and shape of potato chips. They were arranged on edge just like the petals of a rose. I wanted so much to photograph them but given the emotional state of the group, it seemed inappropriate. I couldn't resist eating one. Wow! it was salty like a potato chip. "Potato chips! Anyone want one?" No one responded. They all stood on the bank looking down at me. I came back to help them cross and assist with pulling pulks across. Finally, one by one, the women dropped down and sprinted across.

Once across this branching lead we turned back on our northwest bearing until we were again blocked by the "dreaded black lead." Once again, we followed the shore searching for a place to cross. After some time we came to a section of the lead that was choked with large ice blocks and rubble. With skis off I slid down the bank to check the ice. It was solid. Suddenly Lynne called out, "Matty, look! the far shore is moving!" With adrenaline pumping, I scampered back up in a flash. Yup, the far shore was moving, and moving fast. I figured it was moving at walking speed. Then we noticed a house-size block of ice being dragged along the far shore. Paula whipped out the video camera. Slowly the house-size block of ice sank. With a deep rumble the ice in the lead became a moving river of ice blocks, grinding the rubble into slush. It was an awesome sight to witness these enormous ice blocks tilt, sink and rise among the grinding rubble. We were mesmerized by the invisible power that gave life to the ice. Only moments before I had been standing out there!

North we trudged, negotiating smaller tributary leads until all our options north and northeast were blocked by a network of open leads. Back at our "dreaded black lead" we found another section choked full of ice rubble. We studied it with apprehension. Nothing was moving. I recommended we cross here. The group was hesitant to cross and requested that we ski south to look for a better option. Soon we came to another area of frozen ice rubble and we stopped to scout. I was unclipping my ski bindings when, without warning, the ice came alive and groaned and slammed ice blocks together, causing them to rise and topple. After watching the show of natural power with growing respect for Sedna's unpredictable strength, I recommended we return north to the previous location. We followed our tracks back north. When we arrived, we noticed that here the lead had not been disturbed by the recent movement of ice that we had recently witnessed, which seemed odd, since we could still hear the ice moving to the south. The group waited for Denise and me to check the lead. I studied the ice. I listened. I looked to the north and south for ice movement. While Denise watched for ice movement from the bank, with the throw-line bag in hand, I unclipped from my pulk and ventured across. The lead was safe and I told Denise that our safest option was to cross here.

Denise was very reluctant. My intuition urged me to move out of this hell zone. I pointed out that we did not have much choice: to the north and east were large open branching leads, to the south the lead was on the move and to camp here was dangerous. Denise suggested that we return to our campsite where there was a possible landing strip. "Why?" I replied, "Do you want to end the expedition?" "Yes, that's right," Denise replied. Denise is no wimp. I began to realize how frayed her nerves were from her harrowing swims.

I convinced Denise that it was safer to move forward than to retreat. With reluctance she agreed. When we rejoined the group, I explained, "We must get across this lead and this is the safest place we have seen all day. Lash your skis firmly on your pulk. You can move much faster over ice blocks without your skis on. Unclip your pulk trace. If your pulk jams and the ice starts to move, abandon your pulk. When everyone is ready, we will cross quickly. Keep focused on what you are doing." The women rallied and we made final preparations. When we were all ready, I led the dash across and the team followed in rapid succession: down the bank, over the ice blocks and up the far bank. In less than three minutes we were all across the dreaded black lead!! Emotionally, we were flooded with relief and joyful exuberance, shouting with whoops and laughing at our interpretation.

In those three short minutes the team morale had taken a swing from a deep fearful low to a jubilant high. Extreme mood swings like this are a common indication that individuals are suffering from extreme stress.

With renewed confidence we headed northwest with hopes of leaving this hell zone behind. By mid-afternoon, the winds began to whip up the snow, decreasing visibility. The sky and snow all merged into the same shadowless gray. Without the sun or a horizon to fix my direction on, it was difficult to navigate. To make matters worse, we were forced to zigzag through a maze of more open moving leads. Even the wind refused to be a steady direction indicator as it swirled in eddies behind the ice ridges. This gloomy, overcast, poor visibility day did little to lighten our hearts. We were all quiet and into our thoughts during our breaks. I could tell from looking at the women's faces that the stress of the last two days had worn them down.

The day ended with another adrenaline rush when a high pressure ridge we were crossing suddenly came alive and started to tremble and shake. Denise, Lynne and I were across the pressure ridge when the dragon came alive. Paula was near the top with Sue and Victoria just behind her. In a flash Sue and Victoria dashed past Paula and down the other side. By the time Paula reached the top of the pressure ridge, either her legs or the ice were shaking so much that she was unable to stand up. Denise and I raced back up to help her. Denise grabbed Paula by the arm, screaming, "Paula get up, get on your feet!" as she dragged Paula over the top. I grabbed her pulk trace and pulled her pulk. The pulk jammed. I hopped over the trembling blocks to jerk the pulk free. Just as I freed the pulk, Denise and Paula heaved on the line and the pulk rocketed towards me. I yelled and leaped aside but a ski pole, lashed on top of the pulk, caught me in the shoulder. I twisted away as the pole ripped through the fabric of my parka. That was close! The pole didn't puncture my shoulder but it did tear a large drafty hole in my parka. The roar and trembling of the ice stopped as fast as it had started. With our hearts still pounding, we recounted how hilarious it was to see Paula struggling to get on her feet while Denise, yelling "Get up! Get up," hauled her head first over the top of the ridge and down the other side. Another emotional swing from trembling fear to giddy laughter.

After a long stressful day we found a large, relatively safe pan of multi-year ice to camp on. Here, in our cozy warm tent we appreciate the illusion of safety. The thin nylon walls of the tent block out the reality of our situation: a tent pitched on a thin crust of ice, moved by the whims of the polar currents, opening leads and building pressure ridges of ice across our path.

As the warm soup soothed the knots tied in our guts by the day's little episodes, Victoria shared, "I had a dreadful day. I was fine yesterday after my arctic bath but today, I kept reliving the experience. It has become a haunting nightmare." Yesterday, Victoria had kept up a brave cheerful front. Tonight she admitted, "the experience literally scared the piss and the shit out of me!" Sue guessed her daughter's distraught mood behind her cheerful chatter and has been a solid pillar of support for her.

I sense that keeping the morale up is crucial to this team's safety and forward momentum. If I had Sedna's powers, I would turn down the stress, press the ice pans firmly together, close the leads, stop building pressure ridges across our path and turn the currents to help us achieve respectable northward mileage. Lacking Sedna's powers, I will have to keep a close tab on both individual and group attitude.

A quote by an old friend comes to mind: "Cheer up—it could get worse. So I cheered up, and sure enough it got worse!" (by Dorcas Miller). Not an appropriate quote to share at this time, because, the fact is, in all likelihood it may get worse.

Day 41 Charlie Day 12

APRIL 23, 1997

A.M.	latitude N 86° 12.620'	longitude W 66° 22.571'
P.M.	latitude N 86° 18.037'	longitude W 66° 01.479'
Distance traveled: 6 nm		Total nm from Ward Hunt: 193 nm
Hours traveled: 8.5 hrs.		Total nm to North Pole: 223 nm
Total hours traveled: 246.5 hrs.		Temperature: P.M. -15° C

Sedna must have heard our prayers; she has pushed the ice back together. In comparison to the last few days, we encountered fewer open leads. The pressure that closed the leads has created numerous newly formed pressure ridges of blue ice blocks. To our relief, we did not see, feel or hear any ice on the move. It took a few hours of travel for the group to regain confidence that the ice would remain solid under them. Throughout the day we crossed, on average, one large pressure ridge every hour.

We are over 190 nautical miles from Ward Hunt Island and still the ice has not flattened out. From all the polar books I have read and North Pole adventurers I have spoken with, I got the impression that the ice became smoother 100 nautical miles from land. I wonder if the ice conditions are much rougher this year than in other years. Or is it my imagination that is making mountains out of minor pressure ridges?

Although the ice did not appear to be moving today, we are still drifting at a record rate! Last night we slid .3 nautical miles north and three nautical miles east.

Today was a "shaky" day for Sue as she kept reliving the nightmare she had shared with Victoria. Yesterday, she needed to be strong to support Victoria. Today, Victoria's spirits were up and the nightmare caught and engulfed Sue. This delayed reaction to the accident is interesting. Both Sue and Victoria had handled the accident exceptionally well. After their swim they were chipper, upbeat and optimistic. I suspect this is a basic survival tactic: one must subconsciously know that to fall apart in the face of extreme danger is equivalent to giving up, quitting and ultimately dying. It seems that Sue and Vic pulled on their inner strengths when the situation demanded and let go when they felt safe.

Tonight we talked about the upcoming changeover. Denise and I discussed several points with the group. We touched on the need to make good mileage now that our pulks are lighter and explained what kind of landing strip we must find to keep the First Air pilots happy. We also told the group not to expect the changeover to happen on time.

Day 42 Charlie Day 13

APRIL 24, 1997

A.M.   latitude N 86° 16.721'   longitude W 65° 09.514'
P.M.   latitude N 86° 18.349'   longitude W 64° 39.705'
Distance traveled: 0 nm   Total nm from Ward Hunt: 192 nm
Hours traveled: 6 hrs.   Total nm to North Pole: 224 nm
Total hours traveled: 252.5 hrs.   Temperature: P.M. -14° C

Last night we drifted 1.3 nautical miles south and four nautical miles east. We are caught on a treadmill. We are drifting east faster than we can ski westward. Should we just go north? Richard Weber, veteran of numerous "polar attacks," had warned me that our expedition would be doomed if we were caught in an easterly drift. Will Steger (legendary North Pole explorer from Minnesota) also warned us of this same problem. My intuition tells me to compensate northwest until the drift lets up. I am unsure what to do. The group morale is slipping as we fail to gain miles north. The women worry that they will be letting their relay teammates down by not doing their share of miles north. During breakfast we talked about how imperative it was to keep up individual and group morale. We discussed whether we should travel due north or continue to push northwest in order to regain the 74th meridian.

We decided to push northwest in hopes of getting the next relay team, Delta, off to a better start. We also decided to start looking for a landing strip, as we are nearing the end of Team Charlie's time on the ice.

Today was a mixed day of fast skiing over hard-packed pans with a few medium- to small-size leads and the usual numerous pressure ridges thrown in to break the monotony. Sedna, always the joker, gave us another adrenaline rush. We were taking a break in the lee of a high pressure ridge, munching, drinking and peeing. I was scouting a route 100 meters down the ridge, when I heard the dragon awake with a terrifying rumble right beside the group. I never saw people ski so fast with their pants down! Seconds later, large ice blocks tumbled onto our sheltered rest place.

At 2:30 p.m. we came upon a three-star landing strip. What a miracle! It paced out to the required length. As soon as the tent was up, Denise radioed in, anxious to have the plane bring in Team Delta tonight. Spring is coming and we can't afford to sit in the tent and wait one or two days for changeover. To slip south and east, losing our hard-won miles would be heartbreaking. Today, after six hours of hard work on a northwest bearing, we are at the same latitude as when we set up camp yesterday evening! Plus, we have drifted one degree, 22 minutes (about five nm) east of our last campsite. Our theme song for the day was, "Slip-sliding away, the nearer your destination, the more you're slip-sliding away."

The hard truth is that if this easterly drift continues, we will not make the Pole. It is a very depressing thought. Not to reach our goal after all the time, energy and money that has gone into this expedition; the two years of planning and fund-raising, the selection weekends to find the women with the right stuff, the months of training that the relay women invested, the testing and purchasing of equipment, menu planning, donations of specially designed clothing, and all the hard work by Alfa, Bravo, and Charlie Teams to push the route this far.

Day 43 Charlie Day 14

APRIL 25, 1997

A.M.   latitude N 86° 16.212'   longitude W 63° 24.663'
P.M.   latitude N 86° 14.684'   longitude W 62° 23.522'
Distance traveled: 0 nm   Total nm from Ward Hunt: 190 nm
Hours traveled: 0 hrs.   Total nm to North Pole: 226 nm
Total hours traveled: 252.5 hrs.   Temperature: P.M. -17° C

As we slept, dreaming of a soon-to-arrive plane, our drift was two nautical miles south and five nautical miles east. When will this easterly drift stop? On the morning radio call, Michael relayed that the satellite photos indicated a storm developing later in the day, clearing tomorrow and better weather the following day. We were told no plane today. Michael also told us that the Polar Free and the Dutch were drifting east at about the same rate as we were. The Dutch were heading due north and not compensating for the easterly drift. They felt that they did not need to worry until they slid over the 50th line of longitude. Interesting. Should I head due north as well? My intuition says no.

By early morning the weather had closed in to near blizzard conditions: winds 40–50 kph from the west with visibility less than 1/2 km. We wanted to push on but in our present location, among open leads and shifting pans, it didn't make sense. I declared today a storm day.

Last night, in anticipation of changeover, I washed two pairs of socks and glove liners, wristlets, neck warmer and my capeline one-piece Patagonia suit. I hung my laundry back up this morning to dry along with my damp boot liners. I have stopped wearing VBL liners. The first pair de-laminated and the new pair I requested did not come in on the last changeover.

In anticipation of the changeover, Sue, Victoria, Lynne and Paula are talking about hot showers and the foods they most look forward to eating. This is a little hard for Denise and me. I have not washed my hair in 42 days—yuck. Storm days are great to catch up on little things that I am too tired to do at the end of a travel day. This morning I repaired the rip in my parka (the rip made by the ski pole on the pulk), added two more patches to the palms of my mitts, finished reading my book The Horse Whisperer, and this afternoon wrote letters—and now I am getting caught up in my journal.

After my third hot drink, I went out for another pee and checked the weather. It was definitely getting worse, so there was no chance of moving in the afternoon. Denise slept most of the day. She is feeling a chest cold coming on. Sue and Vic played cards. Lynne and Paula read.

Bad news. I talked to the First Air pilots after lunch. They did not like something in Denise's description of the landing strip. We wonder what; was it statements like; "we need to shovel some bumps" or "sastrugi in wind direction" or "four-meter high ice blocks at one end..." (Sastrugi is the term given to the surface of snow that has become sculptured by the wind. Sastrugi ridges form parallel to the prevailing winds.

These direction indicators have been used as navigation guides for thousands of years by arctic travelers. My favorite forms are the sastrugi that end in a suspended breaking wave—a sea frozen in time.) Morag Howell (First Air base manager) wants us to look for a better runway before she will send the plane!

Emotions erupted after the radio call. "What's the problem here?" questioned Victoria. Someone else interjected, "It is the best landing strip that we have seen in days!" Paula pointed out, "We overheard her telling the Dutch," "No problem, Marc, we'll send the plane now, keep looking for a runway." The women questioned whether they were being treated fairly or was Morag showing favoritism to the Dutch expedition? There was anger, disbelief, frustration and blame being hotly vented and battered about the tent. Denise and I let them pour out their negative energy before bringing the group to face the fact that we must find another runway. We pointed out that our pulks were light and we had enough food and fuel to push some miles north. For Denise and me it was not so hard, as we were not going home for a long time to come. Sue was the one who took the change of plans in stride. She is amazing, strong, steady as a rock—a lovely lady.

For the rest of the day we wrote in journals, exchanged reading books, played cards, took naps, went out to dig more snow blocks to melt, drank more tea, and had to go out for more snow and many more pees.

Day 44 Charlie Day 15

APRIL 26, 1997

A.M.	latitude N 86° 13.975'	longitude W 61° 53.034'
P.M.	latitude N 86° 18.879'	longitude W 61° 42.010'
Distance traveled: 5 nm		Total nm from Ward Hunt: 195 nm
Hours traveled: 9.5 hrs.		Total nm to North Pole: 221 nm
Total hours traveled: 262 hrs.		Temperature: P.M. -15° C

Another overcast, gloomy day; at least the storm let up and we could travel. Today's goal: to find a runway. A nearly impossible task in this flat lighting.

Paula felt sick to her stomach last night and not well this morning. Even with a lightened pulk, she was unable to keep up. At each break she flopped down on her pulk. I had to forcefully insist that she get up to eat, drink and that she put on her parka. I disliked having to be so forceful. While Denise went off to check a possible runway, we divided Paula's load between us and Victoria clipped Paula's near-empty pulk behind hers.

Morale was sinking as we were unable to find a suitable runway. The group had lost its zip and drive. They wanted to go home, now! They had not paced themselves for these extra days and extra miles.

What a day to look for a runway! It was hard to locate a 1/2-kilometer airstrip when visibility was less than 1/2 km. At about 1:00 p.m., we hit "The Alps." We tried to circumvent them to the east but were stopped by open leads. We skied back to the west and I climbed a high ice slab to check the route ahead. Bad news: no easy route around or through. The good news: I could see flatter pans ahead. So we ventured ahead into The Alps, getting bogged down in the deep powder snow that had collected in between the enormous ice blocks. Great shin bashing conditions. Today's joke was, "anyone see a landing strip?" We took photos hauling through hell and laughed at the thought of labeling them: "Team Charlie looking for a runway." These ridiculous jokes lifted our spirits as we helped each other through the tougher obstacles.

We made a great discovery today; we found a slab of ice with shrimp-like krill frozen in it and later an ice block embedded with sand. (After 44 days on the ice, anything new is exciting!) I've read of biologists who take samples of such sand and work out which shore the ice originally came from. I wonder if this ice came from the Northwest Passage? Alaska? or the far shores of Siberia?

In 9.5 hours of searching for a runway we found:
1. one very short flat runway
2. two long bumpy runways
3. one large open lead, big enough to land a float plane.

It was very disappointing to set up camp without a runway. It will mean breaking camp and moving on tomorrow. At least we gained five nautical miles north.

Amazing "luxury items" are turning up in the tent tonight. It turns out that Charlie Team members have smuggled along loads of personal junk, including: large hard-cover reading books, cards, extra cameras, baby wipes, face, body and hand lotions, underarm deodorant. Paula has three stuff sacs of personal junk, Vic has two large sacs. These women continue to amaze me. On Bravo Team, Catherine and Karen both brought teddy bears! (But to be fair, the teddies were well within their one-kilogram limit of personal toys and no one in Bravo had more than 1/2 a sac of personal stuff.)

Changeovers are such emotionally charged times, with wild mood swings up and down. Yesterday, Lynne was a pile of laughs; today she is quiet, introspective and just plodded along. Yesterday, Victoria was a whining spoiled brat, nagging her mother and getting on my nerves. Today, she heroically pulled Paula's pulk and assisted with route-finding. Denise and I are worried about Paula. The stress of the expedition, combined with not knowing when (or if) the changeover will happen, is stressing her to point where she is a liability to the group. We observed this behavior before. She will drag all day, letting others carry her weight, then gets into camp all happy with, "I could have gone on." She's physically capable, but not emotionally resilient. Deep down inside, I question whether she should have been selected to be part of this expedition.

Day 45 Charlie Day 16

APRIL 27, 1997

A.M.   latitude N 86° 18.589'   longitude W 61° 28.822'
P.M.   latitude N 86° 21.130'   longitude W 61° 19.388'
Distance traveled: 1 nm   Total nm from Ward Hunt: 196 nm
Hours traveled: 4.5 hrs.   Total nm to North Pole: 220 nm
Total hours traveled: 266.5 hrs. Temperature: P.M. -16° C

Up at 6:00. The weather was poor. Another overcast day with poor visibility and blowing snow. Denise radioed Resolute for a weather forecast: "might clear in 24 hours."

This morning, Paula informed us that she felt fine, even though she only ate a few bites of cereal. I insisted that she eat 1,000 calories for breakfast to provide her with the energy needed to ski and pull her pulk. She half-heatedly nibbled on bits of dried fruit. This worried me. Her low morale and lack of self-care were signs that she was seriously stressed out. This emphasized our need to find a runway soon in order to avoid the possibility of an evacuation. Moving Paula through this jumble of ice strapped in a pulk was a scenario I wanted to avoid.

We traveled northwest, crossing small leads and climbing over pressure ridges. Denise and I scrambled around, anxiously looking for the routes of least resistance while the group, heads down, plodded along. In Denise's words, "They look like they are going to a funeral." That gave me a good laugh. Emotionally this team checked out on Friday the 25th, the original changeover day. At this pace we were not making good mileage north nor were we finding a runway. Whenever we came to an expanse of whiteness, the group sat on their pulks, while Denise and I paced it out in hopes that it met our runway requirements. I lost track of how many options we checked today. In the flat light, what looked like a two-kilometer runway turned out to be only 150 to 200 meters long and, what looked smooth, was a field of undulating snow dunes.

At 1:30, visibility decreased. We were in an area of potential runways but were unable to see well enough to locate one. I feared that if we continued, we might once again enter a zone of open leads and rubble similar to what we had skied through in the last two days. With this in mind and the fact that the group had lost its zest, Denise and I decided to call it quits for the day. So here we are, camped in a white void. We are out of hot chocolate, the first sign that our food supply is coming to an end.

As I write in my journal, it is an eye-opener to hear the group talk about their fears of missing their flights home, missing a best friend's wedding, concerns about families worrying about them, fears of what to do if we do not find a runway or, running out of food and fuel. When Lynne heard on the radio call, "Not to worry—we can always air drop food and fuel," she really became alarmed. The reality that our situation might come to an air drop shook her. Some of these women are not clued in to the reality of arctic travel. Comments like, "No one told us there was a chance that we'd get frostbite." Did anyone tell them there was a chance that they could fall through the ice? They have read so little about other polar expeditions that it shocked them to find out that our chances of success are less than 50%. Bringing teddy bears on a major expedition is further evidence that some of them think that they are on an adventure holiday with guaranteed arrivals and departures!

What a shock I had this morning! I looked down my long underwear top and noticed that my breasts have nearly disappeared! I know I've lost weight but this is serious. I'm convinced that I've lost over 10% of my body weight, (I started the expedition at 130 lbs.). Before the last re-supply, Denise requested extra rice and mashed potatoes but was told, "No, it's not in the budget." I responded that I would pay for it myself. Rice and potatoes did not arrive in the resupply but instead a note from Mike explaining that he did not want us to eat different food in front of the other women. We asked the women, "Would this be a problem?" "No" they unanimously declared. What is the problem with our SUPPORT TEAM?

All morning I skied obsessed with my starving body. I came to the conclusion that I need more carbohydrates. I'm getting loads of fat (cheese, butter, nuts and salami), plenty of protein (nuts, texture vegetable protein [TVP], extra meat in dinner and lunch salami) and lots of sugar in hot chocolate, juice crystals, dried fruit and McVitie's chocolate squares. What I need are carbos. Tonight I talked to Pen on the radio and requested rice, bread or crackers be sent in with Team Delta. "Denise and I are losing weight, I will pay for it myself," I emphatically expressed to him. After we signed off with "Charlie Polar Relay, listening out," Rick Sweitzer (owner of the Northwest Passage company and leading a group from 88° to the North Pole) came on the radio to say, "Hi, Matty. You are doing great!" and "We'll get our base camp manager in Resolute to send you our extra pita bread." Wow, it was nice to know that someone out there understands and is keen to offer us a little support.

The weather is still not lifting. It's frustrating. I want to make tracks, TO THE NORTH POLE!

Day 46 Charlie Day 17

APRIL 28, 1997

A.M.   latitude N 86° 21.084'   longitude W 61° 18.770'
P.M.   latitude N 86° 21.000'   longitude W 61° 18.000'
Distance traveled: 0 nm   Total nm from Ward Hunt: 196 nm
Hours traveled: 1 hrs.   Total nm to North Pole: 220 nm
Total hours traveled: 267.5 hrs.   Temperature: P.M. -17° C

Throughout the night we took weather watches. Denise was up at midnight to check the weather. Victoria looked out at 1:30 a.m. and woke me up to double check. Yup, it was clearing, a little bit. Hoping that I was making the right decision, I called for a "Rise and Shine." At 3:00 a.m. we radioed Resolute to inform them that the weather was improving and we were heading out to look for a runway. We took down the tent and started checking out the local pans for possible runways. After two hours we returned to a pan situated behind last night's camp. We paced it out, compared notes and declared it suitable. A couple of women came to me and requested that I make the radio call, fearing that Denise might "screw up again." "No, Denise did not screw up, she will make the call." Denise and I have formed a solid working relationship that has grown into a close friendship based on trust and respect. There was no way that I was going to take the radio call away from her and undermine her self-confidence. While the group worked on improving the runway, Denise and I set up the radio. She announced to Resolute that we had a runway, "400 meters long, east-west direction, 50 meters wide, multi-year ice, one-meter high ice blocks at western end. Visibility increasing, 95% cloud cover. Ready for changeover." She wisely failed to mention that we had to shovel a few mounds.

At 7:30 a.m. we talked to a First Air pilot to update him on weather and condition of runway. We radioed again at 11:00 a.m. and learned that they were on their way north! Great news! The emotional roller coaster pushed upward, spirits soared, and wasn't life great. Denise asked, "So, what is the next relay team like?" The response came back, "They're great, you'll really enjoy them, ..."

It suddenly seemed that there was so much to talk about before the plane arrived. We talked of the team's expectations of averaging nine nautical miles a day (they averaged five) and where that came from. There was concern from the women that their relay team had only accomplished 71 nautical miles north. Denise and I were quick to point out that they probably did ski nine nautical miles a day but the south-easterly drift kept pulling back our mileage. We assured them they did a heroic job in not letting the expedition slip over the 50th line of longitude. According to my pre-expedition estimations, we were only 20 nautical miles short of my projected goal for this team. (Both Alpha and Bravo Teams did more miles than I had conservatively estimated.) Twenty miles short was great considering the swimming incident and all the ice movement episodes that we had encountered.

The easterly drift seems to be letting up...a little...maybe. Charlie Team has put the Delta team in an excellent position to push northward.

I spent the afternoon writing letters and finished recording my journal for Paul, Sarah and Eric. At 5:20 p.m. we heard the distant drone of an airplane. The tent suddenly came alive. Stoves were turned off, hot drinks emptied, loose items thrown into stuff sacs, everyone tripping over each other to get out. We left the radio up to communicate with the pilots and our bright yellow and purple tent up to assist the pilots to spot our location. The Twin-Otter circled....and circled...overhead, to the east, then to— "NO NO not south!"—now west...then north. After a half-hour of circling, nearly touching down, then lifting off again, the plane went down to the north and did not rise again. "They're down!" I took a compass bearing on where I last saw the plane. By radio, the pilots told us that they were two nautical miles north of us.

Quickly we dropped the tent, wrapped the radio wires, strapped our skis on and sprinted off. I never saw this team move so fast! Denise, with her hawk eyes, spotted the tail of the plane two kilometers away! We covered the distance in just under 45 minutes. When we crested the last mound we lined up, six abreast and, in true British style, marched onward as team Delta rushed out to meet us. The dismal clouds slipped away and the deep blue skies appeared. Everyone was in a grand party mood. Changeover happened quickly. While our pilots Carl and Amy shoveled bumps on the runway, Juliette (from Team Delta) went through Michael's changeover notes. Michael could not come on this changeover because of the extra fuel barrels needed for the return trip. We learned that David and Rune quit because of "equipment failure." They covered 120 nautical miles in 37 days.

From a nearby ridge, we waved farewell to Team Charlie as they lifted off into the sunshine. The drone of the Twin Otter faded to the south, leaving Denise and me with four new expedition members.

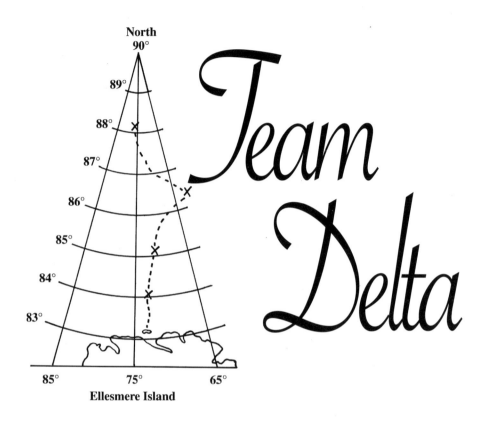

We circled up for introductions and a welcome to "the hardest journey of your life." A check-in on energy levels revealed that we were starting on Empty. Denise and I had had two hours of sleep, with all the radio calls, and the group had had a long trip up. It was 8:45 p.m. so we opted to make camp in order to get an early start tomorrow.

Around the dinner pot, we went through the rituals of getting to know each other. "Where are you from?...Is that near London? Do you have a significant other? Children? What kind of work are you involved in?" It struck me that here we were, thousands of miles from civilization, floating on ice at the top of the world and we were having the same sort of polite casual conversation that we might have at a cock-tail party.

I sorted through the letters and packages of goodies that were brought in by the Delta Team. Not wanting to carry extra weight, I passed around boxes of chocolates. There was a letter from Rita Mathews, a feisty elderly polar research scientist who'd twice been to Baffin Island on adventures with me. Her letter touched me: her vote of confidence in me and her shared understanding of what an arctic journey is really all about.

Dear Matty,

You guessed it, I envy your trip and only wish I were 35 or so and going also. My hat is off to you and I will pray for your every step and safe return. You are so darn able at what you do, you probably will have no trouble at all. However, every expedition I have been on has had something come up that upsets all the plans. Remember that Vladimir Stephansson, who traveled extensively in the North, said that an adventure was only the result of poor planning - so no adventures. He was also a president of the Explorers Club and when you get back you must join. Then maybe we can go on a cruise ship and lecture.

I also just got back from the Antarctic, where Will Steger and I did most of the lecturing. He is going to go back to the North Pole this summer with a device he has made for himself of a canoe on sled runners. He hopes there will be enough open water by July to do a bit of paddling. He will go by himself. Personally, I worry about him; he is now over 50. That's a rough trip and no one has yet succeeded in the summertime.

All the best to you,
Rita

Hum, I'm not so far from 50 myself. (In a couple of weeks I turn 46.)

Day 47 Delta Day 1

APRIL 29, 1997

A.M.	latitude N 86° 21.084'	longitude W 61° 18.770'
P.M.	latitude N 86° 30.000'	longitude W 61° 18.000'
Distance traveled: 9 nm		Total nm from Ward Hunt: 205 nm
Hours traveled: 8 hr.		Total nm to North Pole: 211 nm
Total hours traveled: 275.5 hrs.		Temperature: A.M. -15° C P.M. -17° C

It was after midnight when we finally got to bed so we slept till 8:00 a.m. and were off by 10:30.

When I first met Andre Chadwick, I had a very strong feeling that I had known her in some other time...and I am not sure that I even believe in past lives. After working for many years abroad, Andre now teaches English as a Second Language in London. She is also part of a harmony singing trio. Andre is 33, in excellent physical condition and a person who embraces adventure. In her I sense a balance between sensitivity and strong-mindedness.

Sarah Jones is 28 and a physical education teacher at a private girls' school. She has twice run the London Marathon and has competed in broad-jumping, skills that should come in handy at bounding over wide leads. Last night, Sarah talked openly of the hard times that she has been through in coming to terms with who she is.

Juliette May is a business development officer from Surrey. (I love the sound of English counties and towns, even if I'm not sure where they are.) Juliette is fun-loving and easy to talk to. She is a single mother and, as she explained to Denise and me, is "working class," whereas Rosie is "upper class." How very British.

Rosie (Clayton) Stancer may be from the upper class, but she is the furthest from my image of stiff-upper-lip upper class snob. She bubbles with an invincible zest for living life to its fullest. It's rumored that she was the first woman in the U.K. to bungee jump! Now that is really crazy. Rosie is a joy to have around, always positive and upbeat. Rosie, or Rosebud, as she refers to herself, is a great-niece of the Queen Mother of Great Britain. Denise asked her how many people she would have to knock off to become Queen and she answered, "Oh,...lots."

This group is keen and they bring a refreshing enthusiasm to leap forward into whatever challenges the Arctic offers.

The weather was sunny when we broke camp but suddenly closed in again. We skied over large pans and small pressure ridges until we came to an enormous frozen lead stretching northward to the horizon. Funny thing about the horizon up here: on this flat expanse of frozen ocean sometimes I can see for miles, other times I feel hemmed in. How can this be if the sea is flat? Or does it have undulations like large ocean swells?

All afternoon we skied on the frozen lead and made a good nine nautical miles. We made camp on the shores of the big lead, under gray gloomy skies.

Today on the black ice I was excited to see fern-like crystals. I tasted them to see if their salt content was high. Wow, they were shockingly salty! I was so amazed I turned to Rosie to share the sensation, "Rosie, taste these!" I wonder how much the ratio of salt to H2O has to do with the formation of the crystals.

During the past weeks, frozen leads have offered speedways. Today the snow on the lead was slow to ski on. There was so much friction that it felt as though we were pulling our pulks over wet sand. I have taken up tasting snow on refrozen leads to check my theory that this friction is caused by the salt that has leached up through the sea ice into the snow.

I have been pondering a few other "ice theories." (Matty's Sense of Ice) First, I'm wondering whether the ice will rebound (a little) back to the west after the extreme easterly drift we experienced during the "Big East Drift." Ice and snow have amazing elastic properties. If you have ever seen the snow curl off the eaves of a house, then you know what I mean. Imagine the Polar Sea as a sheet of paper. A current forces the ice to move southeast, and when it slams into the coast of Ellesmere and Greenland it buckles and wrinkles up. Very much like when you push a piece of paper across your desk, it buckles up when it hits your coffee mug. When you release the force on the paper it springs back. Perhaps the ice will do the same. I saw signs of this possibility today along a lead; the ice was wrinkling and rafting along the west bank, in response to a possible rebound effect from the westerly forces that have been pushing us east for the last couple of weeks.

My second observation is that there must be a correlation between the thickness of the ice and the depth of the multi-year snow that has accumulated on top. I have noticed that on the large blocks of ice, heaved up on pressure ridges, the immense slabs have a thicker layer of snow. I wish I had the luxury of time to measure the ratio of ice to snow.

I'd love to take a course on polar ice at the Scott Polar Institute (in Cambridge, England), if they offer such a subject.

Day 48 Delta Day 2

APRIL 30, 1997

A.M.	latitude N 86° 30.368'	longitude W 62° 15.593'
P.M.	latitude N 86° 37.718'	longitude W 62° 44.290'
Distance traveled: 7 nm		Total nm from Ward Hunt: 213 nm
Hours traveled: 8 hrs.		Total nm to North Pole: 203 nm
Total hours traveled: 283.5 hrs.		Temperature: A.M. -15° C P.M. -12° C

We passed the halfway mark! We celebrated with raised mugs and "cheers." These celebrations of our progress are important in sustaining a positive outlook. I am optimistic that the worst is behind us. The pressure ridges are not so high or numerous and with warmer temperatures, our skis and pulks glide more easily. We have won two battles that have stopped many expeditions before us: the extreme cold and horrendous ice conditions at the start and the easterly drift that threatened to sweep us away. Now we must race the coming of summer before the ice breaks up.

Another eight-hour day. During the morning we continued to ski along the big lead and in the afternoon, we were back on small pans and ice rubble. Juliette was having difficulty hauling her pulk—it was too heavy for her to ski it up snow dunes or to reach back and hand-over-hand pull it up. We'll have to shift weights tomorrow.

The heavy weight of our pulks is dragging us down. We must cut any extras we do not need. I asked everyone to go through their personal stuff and see if they could get rid of extra items; share tooth paste, hair brush, hand lotion and to ditch books and unnecessary toys. We decided that tomorrow morning we will sort through the lunch foods and eliminate the food that no one will eat.

On the evening radio call we learned that Polar Free are at 86° 11' N and 63° 46' W. We are 34 nautical miles north of them and 2' west. It seems that they too compensated for the easterly drift. I am worried about them. If they are still hauling 12 hours a day, they should have passed us when they no longer had to double back to haul a second load. They had 52 days of food when we last saw them on March 29. That means they should get to the Pole around May 20th. What is slowing them down? The Dutch are at 86° 59' N and 56° 00' W, which is 22 nautical miles north of us and 24 nautical miles east of us. They must have gotten further north of us when we waited for changeover. Also, we compensated west and they didn't.

Time for bed. I need more sleep to catch up on sleep lost during the last changeover.

Day 49 Delta Day 3

MAY 1, 1997

A.M.	latitude N 86° 37.712'	longitude W 62° 43.843'
P.M.	latitude N 86° 45.358'	longitude W 63° 44.150'
Distance traveled: 7 nm		Total nm from Ward Hunt: 220 nm
Hours traveled: 8 hrs.		Total nm to North Pole: 196 nm
Total hours traveled: 291.5 hrs.		Temperature: A.M. -14° C P.M. -20° C

After breakfast we sorted through the food to lighten our pulks. Everyone had twelve lunches, but we only lightened six lunches in case our appetites increase later. Anything "you won't eat even if you're starving" was thrown to the center of the tent where anyone could trade for something they would eat. The support team back at the Rookery in Resolute would have a fit if they knew that from six lunches we chucked out 4.5 kilograms of chocolate squares and Penguin bars.

Good day today; we moved well over crusty hard-packed snow. It was sunny all day, which lifted my morale—a nice change from the overcast gloom that we have had. I could see for miles and miles and miles. The wings of my spirit could extend to the far horizons.

To help alleviate the monotony, Sarah suggested that we each fantasize about what we would do if we won $1 million dollars then share our dreams in the tent after dinner. Juliette suggested that $2 million would be more fun. After dinner we shared our fantasies. It was rather revealing of our cultural and personality differences. Many said they would pay off parents' mortgages, share the money with brothers and sisters, and give to charities. (I think giving to charities is more of a British value than a North American one.) After hearing everyone else, I felt a bit selfish in my unglobal desires. I shared: take my family to Africa, buy a pair of matching Morgan horses, send Sarah and Eric to a good private school, invest in a retirement fund so that I can retire at 50, buy a cottage on a lake in New Hampshire and build a large ceramic studio, buy Paul surround sound for his home entertainment system, build a bed and breakfast in Iqaluit and get Patsy, (the 1923 Touring Packard that I inherited from my father) fully restored. It's a long wish list, but not really too far beyond what Paul and I could do if we set our minds to it.

Our $2 million discussion was a nice diversion from the usual topics of conversation in the tent. When not discussing the weather or mileage of the day, we usually slide into discussions about body functions or non functions: consistency and volume of bowel movements; efficient methods of unzipping layers for a fast accident-proof pee; what absorbs best, a spare sock or pile neck warmer, when your period arrives unexpectedly. My contribution to the evening conversation was that I have been farting and belching for two days. It's weird; I've been eating the same food for 49 days!

Day 50 Delta Day 4

MAY 2, 1997

A.M.	*latitude N 86° 45.328'*	*longitude W 63° 47.561'*
P.M.	*latitude N 86° 51.701'*	*longitude W 65° 15.480'*
Distance traveled: 7 nm		*Total nm from Ward Hunt: 227 nm*
Hours traveled: 8.5 hrs.		*Total nm to North Pole: 189 nm*
Total hours traveled: 300 hrs.		*Temperature: A.M. -15° C P.M. -15° C*

Today I thought about turning 50 years old in four years and 16 days! What am I doing out here? What really worries me is what I will be doing when I'm 60. Lecturing on cruise ships is looking very cushy and appealing. (Although I'm sure after three days I would be bored.)

We drifted three degrees west last night! This fits with my rebound theory. I hope this westerly drift continues.

Today was a very, very overcast day. Depth perception was one to two meters. It was very much like skiing blind with the help of my ski poles to probe whether the snow was sloping up or down. We traveled north-northwest, on a bearing of 340 degrees, with a magnetic declination of 80° west. Even slowed by poor visibility, we gained seven nautical miles north and four nautical miles west.

Rosie is such a delight to be sharing this adventure with. Nothing seems to shake her un-dauntable, lighthearted spirit. Twice today her pulk bounced down a pressure ridge and knocked her over. Where others (I shall withhold their names) have reprimanded their pulks with nasty words or resorted to beating their pulks with a ski pole, Rosie just hopped up and laughed at herself, "Silly Rosebud."

Radio call days give Denise something to look forward to. In preparation, she writes in her journal exactly what needs to be said and checks in with me and the group before turning on the radio. There is a set procedure to follow, starting with Serial Alpha. Serial Alpha indicates the first item of importance, Serial Bravo the second,

Serial Charlie the third, etc. This procedure is set up to ensure that the most important information is given first in the event that we lose radio contact, and aids us in
communicating all the necessary information. Tonight's radio call went like this:

Denise:	"694, 694, this is Delta Polar Relay. Do you copy?"
Michael:	"Delta Polar Relay, this is 694, you are coming in loud and clear."
Denise:	"Serial Alpha, coms loud and clear."
	"Serial Bravo, general situation okay."
Michael:	"Copy that." (Translates to, "I understand that.")

Tonight Denise skips over Serial Charlie: request for changeover or evacuation,
Serial Delta: medical problems and Serial Echo: equipment problems, as there was
no need to respond on these items.

Denise:	"Serial Fox-trot: Our position is N 86° 51.701' and W 65° 15.480'."
Michael:	"Copy that."
Denise:	"Serial Golf: weather overcast, temperature -15° C, light winds out of north."
Michael:	"Copy that."
Denise:	"Serial Hotel: ice conditions good."
	"Serial India: will continue NNW tomorrow."
	"Serial Juliet: next radio call May 4, at eight p.m."
Michael:	"Copy that. Hold for Nobby."

After Michael's down-to-business information exchange, Nobby comes on to chit-
chat with social news.

Nobby:	"Nobby here. Kohno is at 89° 35'; he hopes to make the Pole tomorrow or the day after." (Wow, that is 25 nautical miles in a day. Either he's pushing really hard or the ice conditions are better up there. I hope the latter.)
Denise:	"Copy that."
Nobby:	"Have a message for Rosie from her great-aunt and her daughter, "God bless you, you are in our prayers and good luck to all of you." (Rosie's great-aunt is the Queen Mother of England.)
Denise:	"We copy that."
Nobby:	"Big news. The Labor party won the election."
	(There was much hooting and cheering, except Rosie was rather quiet.)
Nobby:	"That's it for messages. Keep up the good work, girls. This is 694 listening out."
Denise:	"Thanks, Nobby. This is Delta Polar Relay, listening out."

There was much discussion in the tent about the election. Interesting, but I am not
a political activist. My thoughts are here on the ice, with Kohno and his hope to
travel 25 nautical miles in a day. If only we could make that kind of mileage.

Day 51 Delta Day 5

MAY 3, 1997

A.M.   latitude N 86° 50.790'   longitude W 65° 30.750'
P.M.   latitude N 86° 56.718'   longitude W 66° 49.334'
Distance traveled: 5 nm   Total nm from Ward Hunt: 232 nm
Hours traveled: 8.5 hrs.   Total nm to North Pole: 184 nm
Total hours traveled: 308.5 hrs. Temperature: A.M. -18° C P.M. -15° C

Last night we slipped back south one nautical mile and almost one nautical mile west! We still have 184 nautical miles to go. All day I contemplated about the most direct route to our goal. For the last four days we've traveled on a north-northwest bearing of 340°. The GPS gave us an 86° W magnetic declination.

The sun poured golden light down on us all day. It was a good omen and warmed my spirit. There was magic on the snow and in the air. The moonscape we traveled over glittered like a Christmas card. Ice crystals, suspended in the air, sparkled in the sun like fairy dust. We skied 8.5 hours through more ice rubble to gain only five nautical miles. How disappointing. At this rate it will take us another 37 days to reach the North Pole, for a total of 88 days. But, if we can do six nautical miles a day for 31 days…this is too depressing to dwell on. Maybe we will make the Guinness World Book of Records for the longest trek to the North Pole.

Two more broken bindings today. Andre's Uni-Flex base plate cracked and Rosie's webbing straps wore through. I'm running out of replacement parts. We spent the evening putting together the broken bindings with the few reusable parts we had.

I like Andre; she has a strong sense of righteousness and is willing to live by her convictions. She feels strongly about taking out all our garbage and has volunteered to do so. This has led to an interesting conversation. I just as strongly feel that the best solution for the well-being of our planet is to have the ice crush our garbage. I explained what would happen to our garbage back in Resolute. Andre assured me she would carry it to Edmonton, on route home. (I wonder what they do with their garbage.) Andre and I have come to an agreement, we will respect each other's differences. She will allow me to live by my values and I will let her carry the garbage as long as she is able to continue to haul her share of the group load. Other relay members will have to decide for themselves.

Day 52 Delta Day 6

MAY 4, 1997

A.M.   latitude N 86° 55.981'   longitude W 67° 09.900'
P.M.   latitude N 87° 05.135'   longitude W 68° 49.747'
Distance traveled: 8 nm   Total nm from Ward Hunt: 240 nm

Hours traveled: 9 hrs.   *Total nm to North Pole: 176 nm*
Total hours traveled: 317.5 hrs.   *Temperature: A.M. -18° C P.M. -15° C*

Again the Hot Crunchy breakfast was contaminated with diesel fuel. Yuck. We've been hauling this weight for five days and it's maddening that it makes us sick to eat it!! I belched diesel all morning. Each diesel belch made me want to vomit. Plus, we need the energy. We can't go without eating breakfast.

We skied hard for nine hours on a north-northwest bearing to gain eight nautical miles north. According to the GPS, we traveled 10.6 nautical miles from our last campsite. My guess is that we probably travel 20 - 25% more than what the GPS tells us, if we take into account all the detours around leads and the elevation up and down pressure ridges. To increase our mileage, I decided to increase our travel time by skiing 1-1/2 hours before taking our 15-minute breaks. Today, this reduced the number of breaks by three, increasing our travel time by 45 minutes.

I led for the first five hours with zero depth perception and visibility of 100 to 400 meters. We traveled through ice rubble, over soft snow dunes and across small leads. It was frustratingly slow, as I had to take a bearing every three to five minutes and feel my way over the drifts with extended ski poles. My pulk felt heavier today and my feet were sore, very sore.

The sun came out in the afternoon. Denise led and we made better time over flatter ice pans and small pressure ridges. Again the air was full of suspended ice crystals sparkling in the sun. It was only -15° C and yet it seemed so cold. My hands took 10–15 minutes to re-warm after a break, similar to when it was -30° C. I wonder if it is the ice in the air or if I have lost so much body fat that I am more vulnerable to the cold. Denise felt the cold too.

Tonight I recorded in the Captain's Log under Group Morale:

Sarah: "Most physically challenging day yet."
Andre: "Excellent day until the last hour."
Juliette: "Completely shattered in the last two hours."
Rosie: "Thundered along, belching Rookery gas."

Day 53 Delta Day 7

MAY 5, 1997

A.M.   *latitude N 87° 04.071'*   *longitude W 69° 27.949'*
P.M.   *latitude N 87° 13.243'*   *longitude W 71° 35.240'*
Distance traveled: 8 nm   *Total nm from Ward Hunt: 248 nm*
Hours traveled: 9 hrs.   *Total nm to North Pole: 168 nm*
Total hours traveled: 326.5 hrs.   *Temperature: A.M. -14° C P.M. -9° C*

All day we were battered by easterly winds gusting to 40 kph. According to our wind chill chart, it was -46° C! The wind kept nipping at the right side of my face. I tried to shield my face with my mitt as I skied. Finally, I had to stop and exchange my iced-up neck warmer for a spare one.

The wind and snow have worked with infinite patience to sculpture the sastrugis into suspended waves of snow. In places, there are fields of sculptured sastrugi waves. Skiing across the sastrugi, when the crests are less than one meter apart is fun, as they support us above the trough and reduce the friction on our skis. Skiing over larger sastrugis, spaced further apart, is very difficult as our pulks nosedive to the bottom of the troughs.

All day the winds picked up the loose snowflakes and whipped them into a ground storm. Above me blue skies smiled; around my legs an Arctic blizzard raged. The blowing snows were like a river flowing over obstacles and swirling in the eddies around blocks of ice. I was mesmerized. The snow flowed over my skis and leaped like feathered plumes off pressure ridges. It made me dizzy—the spinning of the earth through the universe.

From this morning's campsite we skied 11.2 nautical miles but only gained eight nautical miles north. Plus, we are experiencing southerly drifts, so if our day drift equals our night drift, then we really covered 12.2 nautical miles. (By comparing our evening GPS position to our morning GPS position we are able to gauge our nightly drift and estimate that it is equivalent to our daytime drift.)

It was a long day for all of us. My feet are whining and complaining. I cut a strip of insulation from my sleeping pad and made insoles to help my feet take the abuse I am putting them through. I'm too tired to continue writing.

Day 54 Delta Day 8

MAY 6, 1997

A.M.   latitude N 87° 12.303'   longitude W 72° 29.366'
P.M.   latitude N 87° 21.922'   longitude W 74° 32.806'
Distance traveled: 9 nm   Total nm from Ward Hunt: 257 nm
Hours traveled: 9 hrs.   Total nm to North Pole: 159 nm
Total hours traveled: 335.5 hrs.   Temperature: A.M. -10° C P.M. -10° C

A.M.
This morning we are at 72° W longitude. I am still planning to work our way back west, to between 74° and 75°. But for today, I've decided to head due north, to gain some good miles north to lift team morale. In this way, I can also check our daytime drift.

P.M.
We are still drifting west! The ice is rebounding from the easterly drift. After heading due north all day, we now find ourselves three degrees west of this morning's camp. At this latitude, three degrees is approximately nine nautical miles!! This is

extraordinary and beyond my boldest hopes. We are back on the 74th line of longitude and we can now aim due north to our goal. This is great...unless we get swept
far away to the west!

Nine hours of skiing gave us nine nautical miles north. A good day indeed. There was
lots of open water today but the leads were small and routes around were easy to find.
However, all this open water is not a good sign. It is only May 5th and we still have
159 nautical miles to go.

Yesterday the wind and ground storm was invigorating. Today it was draining. The
winds blew endlessly in my right ear, stinging my cheek. When I pulled my hood up,
it blew the fur ruff across my face, decreasing visibility and making my visual world
very narrow and small.

Now that our skiing days are longer, there is not much time left in the evenings.
These women are keen and we are usually off, "like a herd of turtles," by 8:30. We
ski until 5:30. By 6:15 we glug down soup and hot drinks, followed by sponge baths,
dinner, melt more snow for more hot drinks, record the day's events in journals, radio
call (on every other night) and usually into our sleeping bags by 9:00 p.m. for a well-
deserved nine hours sleep.

Polar Free has gained on us and we have gained on the Dutch. The Dutch are at 87°
55' N and 59° W. This puts them 27 nautical miles north and 45 nautical miles east
of us. Perhaps the ice conditions to the east are not as good as here on the 74th meridian. Polar Free are at 86° 55' N and 69° W. This equals 16 nautical miles south and
15 nautical miles east of us.

$\mathcal{D}$ay 55 $\mathcal{D}$elta $\mathcal{D}$ay 9

MAY 7, 1997

A.M.   latitude N 87° 20.978'   longitude W 75° 23.223'
P.M.   latitude N 87° 29.106'   longitude W 76° 18.446'
Distance traveled: 7 nm   Total nm from Ward Hunt: 264 nm
Hours traveled: 9 hrs.   Total nm to North Pole: 152 nm
Total hours traveled: 344.5 hrs.   Temperature: A.M. -9° C P.M. -8° C

It's 9:35 p.m. I am writing in my sleeping bag.

It was a very up-and-down day for me. I wonder if it's stress-related. This morning I
led the first five hours under dark and gloomy skies with winds from the northwest
at 16 to 24 kph, poor visibility and at times with a depth perception of zero.

For the first time during the entire expedition I got pissed off. I would shoot a bearing, only to discover 20 steps later that the distant mountain I used as a marker was
an ice lump right in front of me and I had to shoot another bearing. Or, I'd stumble
forward over unseen drifts only to find when I looked up that I'd lost my bearing
marker or it had disappeared behind another unseen ice mound. To add to my frus-

tration, we got into more ice rubble with frozen and partly refrozen leads. With such poor visibility I had no way of knowing if I was leading us through the most difficult obstacles.

Denise is still jittery about going out to test the ice on refrozen leads when she is leading. If I see her hesitate, without a word between us, I go forward. But the responsibility is slowly wearing me down. Everytime I go out to test a refrozen lead, I put my life at risk and then I must make a decision: to cross or not to. I don't think anyone understands the load that I am carrying.

Every break Juliette is "starving" and stuffs her face with lunch snacks as fast as she can. As soon as we are all in the tent, she politely inquires, "Does anyone have any Penguin bars?" We all roll with laughter. I don't know why she is so hungry. Perhaps she has a high metabolism or, being a small woman, she may be burning more calories. At any rate we gladly donate our left-over lunches, and this puts a contented smile on her face.

I too feel hungry all day. One bowl of "Hot Crunchy" plus a coffee and hot chocolate in the morning isn't enough. I have "scientifically" discovered, after 55 days, that the best refueling strategy to keep me warm and moving all day is to eat loads of fats in the morning and sugars later in the day. At the first break I wolf down globs of fatty Palmer ham and top it off with a little something sweet. On the second stop I finish the ham, throw back two handfuls of cashews (which are also high in fat), and grab a sweet to go. By late afternoon, I chew on a strip of beef or turkey jerky (dried meat) and pig out on more sweets like chocolate, fudge or Nanaimo bars. (Geoff and Rosemary Murray, who were on the Baffin Island Expedition with Paul and me in 1990, sent me the Nanaimo bars. Geoff's father had done the same on the Baffin Island Expedition, sending them to each community along the route. They were so good that we ate them all before we got on the trail.)

If Denise and I had not had all these extra treats, cashews, Nanaimo bars, fudge, fruit bread and jerky from friends and family, it would have been very hard for us to keep up our energy and spirits. We are always sensitive to how the women will respond to our eating other treats. So far they have been very supportive and are big-hearted enough to accept it. Even so, we eat our treasured treats discreetly.

It's Paul's and my anniversary today. In the last 14 years of marriage, we have rarely been together on May 7th; one or both of us is usually out leading a trip. I wonder what Paul is doing today. Probably out on the trail with a NorthWinds dog-sledding program or working dogs for the film, Glory and Honor. This is a film featuring Matthew Henson's role in Robert Peary's journey to the North Pole in 1909. Matthew was Peary's black servant.

How I miss traveling with dogs! Bounding over the snow, the dogs fan out (each on its own line) and pull enthusiastically just for the love of pulling. It is instinctual for them to pull. One of the main reasons that Paul and I have made our home in the

Arctic is to run dogs. The type of sled dog that we breed and use is recognized by the Canadian Kennel Club as the Canadian Eskimo Dog, although to be politically correct we refer to them as Canadian Inuit Dogs. (The Inuit of Nunavut dislike being called Eskimo; they find it demeaning.) These dogs are the last indigenous breed to North America. Used by the Inuit for over 2,000 years, they are the dogs that pulled Peary to the North Pole and Amundsen to the South Pole. They are strong, independent and very affectionate. They are not fast, but can pull heavy loads all day, 10 to 16 hours, and do it again the next day, and the next day, and the next day. Paul and I took these dogs on a 4,000 kilometer expedition around Baffin Island. I remember Richard Weber, on a training trip (for his unsupported expedition to the North Pole and back to Ward Hunt Island), took 21 days to ski what Paul and I, on the Baffin Island Expedition, took three days to dog sled! When conditions are ideal, these Canadian Inuit Dogs can cover 50 to 100 kilometers in one day. Yes, I think that Peary made it to the North Pole or very close to it using Canadian Inuit Dogs from northern Greenland. Most everyone who has criticized Peary and the mileage he claimed did not have any dog-sledding experience. I wonder how many days it would take us to reach the Pole if we had dogs. I tried to convince the Women's Polar Relay to take a dog team to haul the group gear. But, like Scott, they wanted to go unsupported! They wanted to be self reliant by "man-hauling." Did they forget that with four resupplies at each changeover we are heavily "supported" by airplanes?

Day 56 Delta Day 10

MAY 8, 1997

A.M.   latitude N 87° 28.811'   longitude W 76° 44.811'
P.M.   latitude N 87° 38.784'   longitude W 76° 54.587'
Distance traveled: 10 nm   Total nm from Ward Hunt: 274 nm
Hours traveled: 9 hrs.   Total nm to North Pole: 142 nm
Total hours traveled: 353.5 hrs.   Temperature: A.M. -9° C P.M. -8° C

Great day. We gained a record 10 nautical miles and had FUN. I needed some time off, so Denise led all day. It was a very overcast day with poor visibility and it started to snow by late afternoon. The lead that stopped us last night and forced us to turn back to make camp was frozen this morning. Conditions enabled us to ski two-by-two and chat. I skied with Rosie during the first leg. We talked about socialism. Juliette and I chatted on the second leg about how she likes Mike and Nobby but finds them "Old Boys' club, upper class, preppy and condescending." While I was skiing with Sarah, she talked about her family and the home that she was creating with her partner. I then skied with Andre and she brought up her issues with the Resolute support team. She was asking them to be accountable for financial matters and they felt that she lacked trust in them. (This was in regard to clothing ordered for them by the expedition that the relay women were asked to pay for. Andre wanted to know what clothing she had bought and why she was now being told that she could not keep it.)

It had been such a fun-filled day until Pen came on the radio this evening, leaving me confused and angry. Pen passed on that he'd had a long talk with Paul and that they, "have worked things out." I was not sure exactly what he was alluding to. In a letter brought in by Team Delta at the changeover, Paul wrote that Pen had held back the final payment of approximately $17,000.00. I hope his "have worked things out" means that Denise and I will get paid for the last third of the expedition! Pen then stated, "I want to reassure you and Denise that I will not be coming on the ice for the last leg nor will I replace you or Denise." He also added: "I think you should be off the ice by May 27." I countered with, "We plan to be at the Pole on May 26." I was riled that he was not even asking me what I thought would be realistic from my perspective on the ice but was giving me his intellectualized armchair opinion.

Pen went on, "Paul thinks that you should pick up the pace and really start pushing." That really upset me! What was I suppose to push with? I had four clients new to arctic travel. They were performing exceptionally well and giving their heart to this expedition. Had Paul forgotten the Everest disaster where seven clients died because the leaders took too many risks in trying to get their clients to the top[4]?

After Pen signed off, conversation exploded in the tent. The women wanted to know what Pen meant by, "I will not be coming on the ice for the last relay leg nor will I replace you or Denise?" I explained that in the negotiations between NorthWinds and Pen/Caroline, they had insisted that Pen had the option of coming on the ice for any or all the sections of the relay. I had strongly objected to this but Pen and Caroline were adamant. In the end, the contract stated that Pen could join for the last section only. The contract read in part:

The Guide's professional services, responsibilities and rights include:

c)   Guiding services for the Participants for the entire journey from Ward Hunt Island to the North Geographic Pole

d)   The Guides accept that Pen Hadow may also participate in the last leg of the journey, if requested by his client(s), the relay squad

This was a shock to the Delta team as they had not been informed of any such thing. (Caroline had assured me, when we met in January in Iqaluit, that this clause in the contract was okay with the other expedition women.) I was bombarded with questions: "But I thought this was a women's expedition! Am I wrong? Would it be a women's expedition if Pen joined? How come we were never informed of this?" I politely explained, "The Women's Polar Relay would lose its opportunity to become the first women's expedition to the North Pole if a man joined." They were furious.

They also wanted to know what the issue was around replacing Denise and me. I answered that Pen and Caroline did not want the leaders to travel the entire way to

---

4 The truth I discovered, when I got home, was that Pen had tried to get Paul's support for telling me to "really start pushing." Although Paul agreed that it would be good to push, he emphatically expressed to Pen that it was up to Matty to make that decision. Paul told Pen that Matty had the experience and wisdom to know when to push and how hard to push in order to reach the North Pole safely. She was on the ice and would make the proper decisions.

the Pole since they felt it could belittle the relay women's accomplishments. I explained that during contract negotiations, we had insisted that Denise and me guide the entire journey from Ellesmere Island to the North Pole and that Pen had agreed. I did not express my gut feelings, but my thoughts on the matter are that Pen and Caroline had planned to take Denise and me off the expedition for the last leg of the journey. This would ensure we did not steal the "spotlight" from Caroline and Pen as the "leaders" of the expedition. For Pen to say "will not replace you or Denise" makes me sick to my stomach. The contract states clearly that we are guiding the entire journey.

I am upset. I need to go out for a walk and get some fresh air and let go of all this negative baggage. I wish I could talk to Paul.

Day 57 Delta Day 11

MAY 9, 1997

A.M.   latitude N 87° 37.819'   longitude W 77° 13.355'
P.M.   latitude N 87° 46.613'   longitude W 76° 53.589'
Distance traveled: 8 nm   Total nm from Ward Hunt: 282 nm
Hours traveled: 9.5 hrs.   Total nm to North Pole: 134 nm
Total hours traveled: 363 hrs.   Temperature: A.M. -6° C P.M. -6° C

A.M.

I did not sleep well. I kept going over things said and not said on last night's sched call. It turns out that no one slept well. This morning we discussed our feelings and our reactions. Last night our spirits were soaring when we learned that we'd done a record ten nautical miles. The radio call dragged our spirits down into the pits. It's nice to know that I am not the only one who was upset by Pen's communications.

Most of the night I thought whether we can push the team more. This morning I discussed it with Denise. She thinks we should try traveling for ten hours a day and see what the result is. A nine-hour day is already a long day and most of the group is knackered long before we arrive at our campsite. In the afternoon while Denise leads, I ski at the back and assess how often the women fall, how long it takes them to struggle up or how often they need help to haul their pulks over pressure ridges. This assessment helps me determine whether I should increase or decrease the length of our travel day. I worry about pushing beyond the safety line. The repercussions of passing over this invisible line may result in a minor incident, like falling through the ice, turning into a major disaster because everyone is so exhausted they can't deal with the situation properly. I also know, from 23 years of experience leading groups in the wilderness, that we will cover more miles in the long run if we don't go over the burnout point. It's the same working with a dog team. If I push the dogs too hard one day, they may not bounce back for two to three days. I am ultimately responsible for the safety of these women and must act accordingly.

We have five more days with Delta if all goes according to plan. Pen told us on the radio call that the First Air pilots are worried that runways are harder to find further north and that Team Echo will be ready to come out on the 13th, one day earlier if necessary.

The sun is out. Yeah! My solar batteries are recharging. The sun even feels warm. Back in March the sun provided light but not warmth; now I'm worried that the snow might turn into wet cement and the leads will open. This warmth also bring out body smells. As Juliette says, "The tent smells of small animals." Like stinky hamsters. Sarah, on snow melting duty, just gave us a warning, "Three water bottles to go." That means about ten minutes before the stoves are shut down and the tent is dropped. Let's go to the North Pole! I've decided to travel 9 1/2 hours today and evaluate the energy level at the end of the day.

P.M.

The ice conditions were flatter today and skis and pulks were actually gliding! This was another first. We skied 9-1/2 hours and covered eight nautical miles. In the late afternoon, we came to a four- to five-meter lead running east-west. We turned east as it looked like the more promising direction to locate a crossing. As we skied along I heard "Plop!" I turned to look at the lead and saw a ripple of extending rings as if someone had thrown a rock. No one was behind me. I waited; then not three meters away, the head of a ring seal popped up and blinked at me. I was so excited that I yelled, "seal, seal seal!!" Which of course scared him down. A minute later he popped up again for a better look at these strange creatures. He swam alongside of us as we skied along the lead, silently watching with big dark eyes.

We gave up looking for a bridge over the lead and made camp at 6:00 p.m. Perhaps if we are patient, Sedna will close the lead tonight. It is noticeably colder camping by this open lead. A chilly damp, cutting cold, like winter in New England.

Rosie entertained us after dinner with "A day in the life of a British debutante." She had us holding our sides with laughter. What a fun evening. I enjoy this group. The humor and laughter is great.

Day 58 Delta Day 12

MAY 10, 1997

A.M.   latitude N 87° 45.253'   longitude W 76° 55.648'
P.M.   latitude N 87° 51.741'   longitude W 75° 32.451'
Distance traveled: 5 nm   Total nm from Ward Hunt: 287 nm
Hours traveled: 9.5 hrs.   Total nm to North Pole: 129 nm
Total hours traveled: 372.5 hrs. Temperature: A.M. -10° C P.M. -10° C

Another overcast, gloomy, hard-to-navigate day. Sedna froze the lead that halted us last night. The new ice was a rubbery three centimeters thick. We crossed in slow motion, slowly sliding one ski at a time and gently shifting our weight from ski to ski. I let out my breath when all six of us were across.

Overall, the ice was flatter and there were fewer towering pressure ridges. We should have been speeding along but were slowed by numerous open leads. Most of the smaller stream-width leads could be stepped over with skis. The wider river-wide leads had to be scouted to find a narrows or a bridge of ice floaters. Once a suitable crossing was found and the ice was tested, we weighed the risk of crossing and, if safe, scooted across.

At 5:30 we were again stopped by a large east-west lead. We took this as a message from Sedna that it was time to make another chilly camp. Tonight we talked to Caroline on the radio. She will be coming in with the final relay team, Team Echo. We exchanged thoughts on reducing weight by cutting back on clothing and equipment. At the end of the radio call she asked exactly what Denise and I were carrying in our pulks. Denise told her we would write this down and tell her tomorrow night. (We radio in every night before changeovers.)

The other teams on the ice are:
Dutch 88° 14' N and 60° 00 W (about 23 nautical miles north of us)
Polar Free 87° 05' N and 72° 00 W (about 46 nautical miles south of us)

Since May 6 we have gained four nautical miles on the Dutch, and pulled 30 nautical miles ahead of Polar Free. This is exciting. It confirms that we are really doing great! I can't help feeling proud of these women who, with no previous winter camping skills or arctic experience, are gaining on a group of experienced expedition men! I believe that we are succeeding because we are traveling and camping with style. Traveling in style to me means that we are taking care of ourselves: eating before we are starving, drinking before we are dehydrated, stopping before we are exhausted. It means that we have the extra energy to help each other over the ice and support each other emotionally when needed. It means having a warm tent to look forward to during cold days. It means being able to dry our wet mitts, hats, neck warmers. It means keeping up our morale by taking sponge baths, brushing teeth and hair and taking time to repair items of clothing or equipment. It means not dreaming of being somewhere else. Doing it in style means celebrating the joy of living on the polar ice with love and laughter.

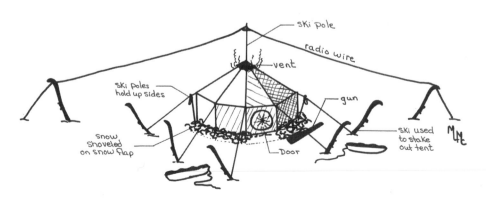

Day 59 Delta Day 13

MAY 11, 1997

A.M.   latitude N 87° 50.894'   longitude W 74° 36.063'
P.M.   latitude N 87° 57.682'   longitude W 74° 13.525'
Distance traveled: 6 nm   Total nm from Ward Hunt: 293 nm
Hours traveled: 10 hrs.   Total nm to North Pole: 123 nm
Total hours traveled: 382.5 hrs. Temperature: A.M. -12° C P.M. -9° C

We skied ten hours today. My feet are killing me. I think about Geoff Murray, whose feet hurt all summer after the Baffin Island Expedition. I need to lighten my pulk. Denise, Andre and I are pulling the heaviest pulks. It's time to redistribute the weight more equally.

We saw what might have been polar bear tracks today. There were eight to ten large bear-like prints in the snow. They were very wind-blown.

Another radio call tonight. Pen explained that First Air needs to put in a cache of fuel on the ice at 86° before they can bring in Team Echo. The Twin Otter plane cannot carry enough fuel to fly from Eureka to here and back without refueling. The pilots have asked us to radio in weather updates a.m. and p.m. We can also expect the winds over the next two days to be at 40 kilometers out of the southwest.

After Pen finished, Caroline came on the radio and drilled Denise on exactly what Denise and I have in our pulks. She wanted to know specifically how much camera equipment I had. She stated that the five-kilogram box that Paul sent me with Delta was all camera equipment and that I had taken it all. How exasperating. (In the box were letters that I burned, chocolate, rice and noodles that I shared with the group, ten roles of film for this relay section, a new lens cover to replace the one I broke, a small Yashica camera to replace the Advantex camera that the expedition ran out of film for and a lens that I promptly returned.) During yesterday's radio call, Denise said, "I am carrying group gear plus two breakfasts and Matty carries two gallons of fuel." She meant to say that I carried group gear plus two gallons of fuel. But Pen and Caroline misconstrued this to mean that I was only hauling two gallons of fuel because I was carrying so much personal camera equipment. This smear on my reputation left me very frustrated.

Radio calls have become such a low point in the day.

Day 60 Delta Day 14

MAY 12, 1997

A.M.   latitude N 87° 57.263'   longitude W 74° 27.534'
P.M.   latitude N 88° 07.441'   longitude W 75° 15.462'
Distance traveled: 10 nm   Total nm from Ward Hunt: 303 nm
Hours traveled: 10 hrs.   Total nm to North Pole: 113 nm
Total hours traveled: 392.5 hrs. Temperature: A.M. -10° C P.M. -4° C

A.M.

I didn't sleep well last night. I was wide awake with stirred-up thoughts from Caroline's radio conversation. Even with ear plugs, Rosie's melodic snoring next to my ear kept me up. I considered dragging my sleeping bag outside but it was snowing. I also had visions of a polar bear finding me a delicious snack, feathery on the outside, mushy on the inside. A good excuse for my lazy reluctance to get out of my warm sleeping bag and move.

Day 60 of Hot Crunchy—I'm getting sick of it. I eat it cold, but the thick dusting of milk powder is nauseating. (At home, the smell of mixing powdered milk makes me want to puke.) When I get the bottom of the breakfast bag with all the powdered milk, I fill my bowl with hot water, rinse the cereal and pour off the disgusting milk. But then the hot water accents the diesel fuel taste and I can't eat it.

Rosie sits beside me in the tent. As usual she has her place mat out with mug and bowl in proper position. Her place mat is the 30-centimeter square piece of ensolite used to keep our feet off the snow when sitting in the tent, a gift left from Team Charlie.

P.M.

We had a good day today. All morning we skied in a bright magical ice-fog. The haze gave a soft diffused light. Sounds of voices and crunching skis were muffled. The windless air gently caressed my face. Ahead, the line of skiers faded and disappeared soundlessly, as if into the "Mists of Avalon." We crossed the 88th degree. Only two degrees to go. Yeah!

We crossed Ohbasna's solo ski tracks. He started from the Russian side of the Polar Sea and is heading to Ward Hunt Island. We think he was at the Pole a couple of days after Kohno on the 4th of May[5]. If so, he must be doing 20 nautical miles a day! No pulk tracks, so he must be carrying a backpack. Sarah felt that his tracks were "part of his history, and that if I skied in them I was defacing his art." Denise felt differently; she said that she enjoyed skiing in his tracks, that they gave her energy.

We followed Ohbasna's tracks all morning. I wonder if it's proper arctic etiquette or playing by the rules to follow another's tracks. Anyway, his track led us due north and gave Denise and me some much needed time out from navigating responsibilities. As the group set the pace, Denise and I brought up the rear. We talked about what equipment we could ditch to lighten our pulks for the final dash to the Pole. We decided to send back one shovel, one stove and our VBL sleeping bag liners. (At the last re-supply, we ditched our insulated pants and down parkas.)

In a maze of small open leads and ice rubble, we gave up on following Ohbasna's trail as it seemed to lose itself in circles. In the afternoon our trail wove between open cracks from pan island to pan island. These cracks were three- to four-meters deep, which told

5 Ohbasna was never able to make it to the North Pole. He camped a few miles away and the next morning had drifted miles away. All the next day he tried to reach the Pole, only to slide away again that night. He gave up and continued on to Ward Hunt Island.

us that we were traveling on old multi-year ice. On most of these cracks we were able to find a narrows to ski over. A couple of times, we had to broad-jump. Sarah, our professional broad-jumper, volunteered to jump first and catch us on the other side as we tottered on the brink. I was thankful Sarah was on the far side to help those of us with shorter legs. It would have been difficult to rescue someone had they fallen in.

My stomach gets butterflies when I look down two to three meters into cold black water when I step over these crevasse-like cracks. The best technique is to approach the crack at right angles. Stop at the edge and pull your pulk up to ensure that you have enough slack in your pulk line so that you don't get jerked off balance in mid step. Next, shuffle to the lip and with your ski pole test that there isn't an overhang of snow at the edge of the crack. Now, move your ski tips over the void and get both boots to the lip. Lean forward to plant both ski poles on the far side. Next take a giant step so that your foot is centered over the crack, with the tip and tail of your ski on either bank. Cautiously transfer your weight onto this ski and pray that your ski is strong enough as it bends under your weight, suspended in space. With your other ski, gingerly take a LARGE step so your foot gains the far edge. One more carefully balanced step and you're over. Almost. Now your pulk has to follow. Check that it is perpendicular to the crack. Run like hell and pop it over. The "oops" are: 1) the nose of the pulk plows into the opposite bank, bringing your forward motion to a jerking, back-flipping halt, or 2) the front clears but the back drops into the crack.

This is day 14 with Team Delta. They are scheduled to be on the ice two more days, but with the warning from First Air that runways this far north may be difficult to find we will start looking tomorrow.

Day 61 Delta Day 15

MAY 13, 1997

A.M.   latitude N 88° 06.243'   longitude W 75° 25.972'
P.M.   latitude N 88° 10.726'   longitude W 75° 36.217'
Distance traveled: 3 nm   Total nm from Ward Hunt: 306 nm
Hours traveled: 5 hrs.   Total nm to North Pole: 110 nm
Total hours traveled: 397.5 hrs.   Temperature: A.M. -6° C P.M. -7° C

Yesterday we skied until 7 p.m. and got to bed late, and so we slept until 7:00 a.m. in order to get our needed nine hours of sleep.

We skied fast over flat pans of year-old ice that extended north to the horizon. Although the surface appeared smooth, the ice was riddled with a lace-work of deep cracks and leads. At our 1:00 p.m. snack break, Denise and I climbed up a mountain of ice rubble to scout the route ahead and to look for potential runways. We returned to the group with: "The bad news is that to the north of us stretches endless ice rubble. The good news is that to the southeast there are numerous landing strip possibilities." We divided into reconnaissance groups to pace out runway options. At 3:30 p.m. we set up camp and radioed that we had a runway and that the sun was coming out. Our luck was shining! Could changeover really be this easy? The group was elated. Denise warned them not to get their hopes too high with changeover; anything could happen.

We were told that Team Echo, the last of the relay teams, was scheduled to depart Resolute at 6:00 p.m., land in Eureka at 8:30 to refuel and then on up to us between midnight and 4:00 a.m.

Denise and I performed our changeover rituals; we took sponge baths, Denise washed her hair, we washed underclothes, made repairs to clothing and wrote letters. To keep us entertained, Sarah introduced us to a "Life" game. She gave each of us a piece of paper with six simple shapes drawn on. She instructed us to draw on the shapes the first thought that came to mind. When we finished, she explained that the circle was ourselves, the two slanted lines were our life, the box our home, the X our family, the triangle was our spirituality and the S was our sex life. In the circle, I drew a contented face with eyes closed and smiling mouth. I drew skis out of the two lines that represented My Life. The square box I made into a simple box house with lollipop trees. My Family was represented by two crossed swords for a Scottish sword dance. A snow-topped mountain with me standing on top with arms uplifted reflected My Spirituality. My Sex Life was a snake. I wonder what that means!

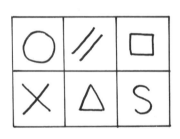

Sarah's Game

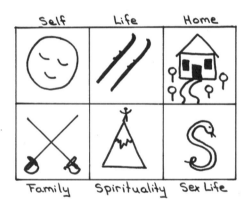

Every two hours we called in the weather. At 8:00 p.m., we learned that the Twin Otter was having problems with a fuel filter. At midnight, Carl, the veteran Swiss-German pilot with 23 years of arctic flying, said he had to turn back. He could not land at the fuel cache because the runway was no longer good and he couldn't locate another runway nearby. He said he was sorry but they were returning to Eureka and would not be able to make another attempt until 11:00 a.m. Bummer.

Day 62 Delta Day 16

MAY 14, 1997

A.M.   *latitude N 88° 10.184'*   *longitude W 76° 01.281'*
P.M.   *latitude N 88° 10.146'*   *longitude W 76° 15.526'*
Distance traveled: 0 nm   *Total nm from Ward Hunt: 306 nm*

Hours traveled: 0 hrs.   *Total nm to North Pole: 110 nm*
Total hours traveled: 397.5 hrs.   *Temperature: A.M. -11° C P.M. -10° C*

I had the luxury to sleep in this morning until my bladder forced me out of my cocoon. Bad news, the weather had closed in again. Denise's 11:00 a.m. radio weather report: "-6° C, south wind, snowing, visibility 1 kilometer, poor definition."

I spent a relaxing morning writing more letters and napping in and out of dreams. I didn't have the energy to worry about what I cannot control: the weather, when First Air will decide to try again, how much food remains (one dinner, two breakfasts and an assortment of lunch stuff), or liters of fuel (15 liters)...and that we are not making miles north. C'est la vie.

Lunch of hot soup with melted cheese, such a treat. I threw a couple of chunks of butter into my steaming soup (to add calories) only to discover, to my chagrin, that the butter was contaminated with diesel fuel. I had to throw out my soup. This contaminated food is truly a low point for me. I felt hungry and sorry for myself all day. Dinner, without the addition of extra noodles or rice, amounted to one not-so-large bowl. (We have been adding the extra rice and noodles sent in for Denise and me to the group meal but have run out.) Juliette licked her bowl clean to get every last morsel.

I often fantasize about food: fruit salads with raspberry yogurt, shredded coconut and walnuts, hot toast with melted butter, fresh brewed coffee, homemade bread right out of the oven, strawberry-rhubarb pie with real whipped cream, (this is fun), caribou steak with baked potatoes and sour cream, spinach salad, Caesar salad, a bowl of tender little Greenland shrimps, pizza with extra mozzarella, pepperoni and olives, artichokes dipped in melted lemon butter, lemon meringue pie, brown sugar fudge, maple sugar candy, (no chocolate, I'm sick of it), cream of broccoli soup, borscht soup, pumpernickel bread, black German bread, Mom's sticky buns, sun-ripe pears and peaches, fresh broccoli and cauliflower slightly steamed with a caraway cheese sauce, a platter of fresh veggies and dip, toll house chocolate chip cookies still warm...Food, Glorious Food.

At 7:00 p.m. we radioed First Air in Resolute with a weather update of "continued poor conditions." Morag (First Air base manager) sounded cheerful. She said that she was leaving for her four-week break and would not be in Resolute when Denise and I returned.

At 7:30 p.m. the sun broke through. We got excited and tried to radio through every half-hour to report "good weather for changeover." It was infuriating that no one was manning the radio either at First Air or at the Rookery. I also sent four Argos messages: "good for changeover." Finally at 11:30 I got someone at First Air who said to call back in 15 minutes while he looked for Morag. Fifteen minutes later, he said, "Morag wants you to call at 7:00 a.m." This is crazy! It's sunny and we can see for miles. What is the problem?

For the last five nights the sun has come out between 8:00 p.m. and 2:00 a.m. First Air knows this, we've told them. Yet they do not make any attempt to be ready for this window of good weather.

⸺ Day 63 Delta Day 17 ⸺

MAY 15, 1997

A.M.   *latitude N 88° 10.170'*   *longitude W 76° 27.638'*
P.M.   *latitude N 88° 10.304'*   *longitude W 76° 39.488'*
Distance traveled: 0 nm   *Total nm from Ward Hunt: 306 nm*
Hours traveled: 0 hrs.   *Total nm to North Pole: 110 nm*
Total hours traveled: 397.5 hrs.   *Temperature: A.M. -7° C P.M. -7° C*

Still waiting for changeover. Our 7:00 a.m. radio call with the weather update: "visibility under 1 kilometer, high cloud cover, light snow falling, -7° C, no wind, no contrast." Morag requested an 11:00 a.m. radio call. I explained to her that for the last five nights we've had a five- to seven-hour window of sun in the late evening and poor weather during the day. She asked me to hold...then came back asking us to radio at 6:00 p.m. or anytime the weather cleared and stabilized. At 10:00 a.m. it was starting to clear but we were unable to get through. No one was manning the radio again!

Another sleep-in, another breakfast of contaminated Hot Crunchy and another hot drink of coffee followed by a second cup of mocha. The morning continued with tea, followed by a pee and more tea. I've finished washing, repairing and writing. Denise, Andre, Sarah and Juliette have been playing Hearts for two days! Denise and Sarah refuse to quit until they beat Andre, who continues to hold the lead. I'm bored, my toes are cold and I'm still hungry! I'm sounding like Sarah and Eric when they get whiny, "Mom, I'm bored, there's nothing to do, I'm hungry."

The weather continued to clear. By late afternoon when we were able to get through on the radio the weather had closed in again. We were asked to call in the morning.

⸺ Day 64 Delta Day 18 ⸺

MAY 16, 1997

A.M.   *latitude N 88° 10.334'*   *longitude W 76° 31.421'*
P.M.   *latitude N 88° 10.676'*   *longitude W 76° 16.032'*
Distance traveled: 0 nm   *Total nm from Ward Hunt: 306 nm*
Hours traveled: 0 hrs.   *Total nm to North Pole: 110 nm*
Total hours traveled: 397.5 hrs.   *Temperature: A.M. -8° C P.M. -10° C*

Up at 7:00 a.m. to call in our local weather to Morag at First Air: "-5° C, overcast, light snow, no wind, 1/2 kilometer visibility." She asked me to call back at 9:00 a.m.

At 9:00 I called to report: "The sun is out! Excellent visibility!" Morag said they did not have a plane available; call back at 6:00 p.m.! What is going on down there? They promised to have a plane ready as soon as we had good weather. Now when the sun comes out, no plane.

At 11:00 a.m. I tried to call Michael to tell him the sun was shining and ask if he knew what was up with First Air. There was no answer but Paul Schurke came on the radio to say hello. Paul was further south on Ellesmere Island. He was basking in the sun waiting for the second plane to bring in his clients. I asked if he had dogs. "Yes, they are stretched out in the sun" was his reply. Paul co-led the "North to the Pole" expedition with Will Steger in 1985. They traveled with dog teams but without air resupplies and were successful in reaching the Pole.

Michael came on the radio after. I passed on that we were "sun bathing." "Sorry," he explained, "No plane." I guess the planes were being used to shuttle Paul's dogs and clients to Ellesmere.

After the radio call, Team Delta started firing off nasty comments about Morag. I am sure that many of their feelings were projected frustrations of missing flights home, running out of food, not understanding why the plane wouldn't come when the sun was out. They talked about how, when they were in Resolute waiting to come on the ice, that Morag had seemed to be obstructing Team Charlie's changeover. They told Denise and me that it wasn't our runway that was in question but politics between Morag and Pen.

Morag had been part of the selection weekends at the beginning of the project. I was told then that she was going to be part of the support team in Resolute as our communications manager and that she was the best communications person at high latitudes. Last January First Air offered her the Resolute base manager position and she accepted. Although she would no longer be working specifically for the expedition, she promised to give us first priority on planes for changeovers.

I hope the Pen / Morag / First Air politics don't cause this expedition any more serious problems! At the 9:00 p.m. radio call we were told no plane tonight. They will send a plane to Eureka at 6:30 a.m. We are to call in the weather at that time and if the report is good, they will bring in Team Echo. If the weather is bad, they will drop ten days of food and fuel.

On the radio, Joost, the manager of the Dutch Expedition, said hello and that he had had a great dog sledding trip with NorthWinds in Iqaluit. (NorthWinds ran a dog sledding program for the expedition's relatives and key sponsors.) The Dutch are at 89° 09' N and 69° 21' W.

I'm tired of sleeping, writing in this journal and eating trail food. We are now out of trail food, so that solves that. I want to get going north, get to the North Pole so that I can go HOME!

In the early hours of the morning the plane finally came north. It has become a well worn joke that, "the plane never comes when the sun is out, only when we are nearly out of food and the sky overcast." At any rate, we were overjoyed to see the plane circling over us through partly overcast skies. This time the pilots even liked our runway, marked off with pulks and sleeping bags on skis. After touching down and lifting off to test the runway, they set down and motored over to our tent.

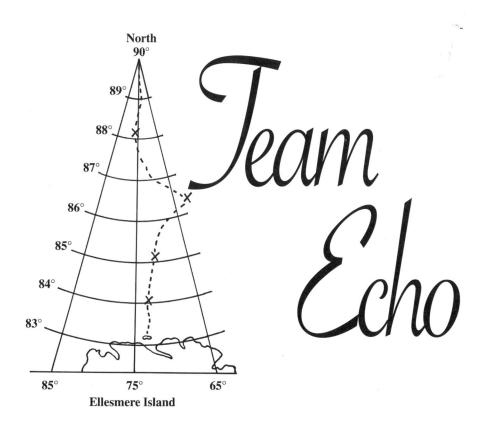

North
90°
89°
88°
87°
86°
85°
84°
83°

85°   75°   65°
Ellesmere Island

Jeam Echo

Day 65 Echo Day 1

MAY 17, 1997

A.M.   latitude N 88° 11.257'   longitude W 76° 46.940'
P.M.   latitude N 88° 19.965'   longitude W 75° 25.959'
Distance traveled: 9 nm   Total nm from Ward Hunt: 315 nm
Hours traveled: 6 hrs.   Total nm to North Pole: 101 nm
Total hours traveled: 403.5 hrs. Temperature: A.M. -8° C P.M. -10° C

After brief introductions, Denise and I checked food and fuel quantities, replaced two poorly functioning stoves, and picked up our personal re-supply packages. There was a round of farewell hugs before Sarah, Andre, Rosie and Juliette climbed up the ladder into the belly of the Twin Otter. We on the ice stepped back as the engines roared and whipped up the snow. The plane lumbered down the runway, turned, bounced along the snow and lifted off, carrying the Delta team homeward. One hundred and ten nautical miles to go with the last relay team. I hope for an easy dash to the Pole but fear that Sedna may bring spring all too soon.

It was mid-morning when we strapped on skis with Team Echo and headed north at a surprisingly fast pace. Surely, I thought, they can't keep up this pace. But every time I stopped to shoot a bearing, they were right behind me.

In six hours of travel (we did not have a full day because of changeover) we gained nine nautical miles north. This was accomplished with a little help from the rebounding ice, which is pushing us northward at about two nautical miles in 24 hours. Incredible!

I am a little apprehensive about working with Caroline Hamilton—Caro, as her friends call her. Caroline is 33, and a tall slim woman. The Women's Polar Relay is her dream and this is very much Caroline's expedition. For two years she has been the driving force behind the selection of these "ordinary women" and raising the $600,000.00 to get the expedition heading to the North Pole. Now she is here on the polar ice with some of her closest friends—who naturally look to her for leadership. Even though Caroline has absolutely no arctic experience to lead this group, I sense a strong undercurrent of competition.

Zoë Hudson lives with Caroline in London. She is 30, a sports physiotherapist completing her Ph.D. Zoë puzzles me. She has run the London Marathon twice and yet she is a heavy smoker. She doesn't like camping but here she is camping on snow and ice. One moment Zoë is bursting with zest and the next she is in a dark, pouting mood. I'm never sure whether she will laugh or throw daggers.

Pom Oliver is 44, and lives with her husband in Buckinghamshire. She works as a film producer and, with Caroline, is also involved in film financing. I get the impression that Pom is from "old money." Her description of "the cottage" sounds like a country estate. Her off-handed remarks about remodeling sound extravagantly decadent.

Lucy Roberts is 27 and lives in West London. She was a journalist at The Independent and is now a lighting designer. Lucy is also a marathon runner and, oddly, also a heavy smoker. Lucy is petite, with short cropped bleached blond hair. She positively hates dumb blond jokes. When I asked how she managed to be with the elite Echo team, she explained that she helped to raise the most funds for the expedition.

This group objects to following the camping routines developed by the earlier teams. They have decided to do camp chores at random and also to rotate sitting and sleeping places in the tent. I wonder if this is their way of developing their own individual team-ness, or a way to demonstrate that they are not part of the teams that labored before them—or is it a subtle rejection of my leadership?

Denise and I spent the evening reading mail and opening packages from family and friends. I received letters from Paul, Eric, Sarah, Pen, Michael, and Kay. Kay, my old college friend, sent me some New England jokes, some bread that she made, and raspberry tea. The support from home and friends is deeply appreciated. Michael wrote a three-page letter in which he warned me that I will have to deal with some issues with Caro.

Day 66 Echo Day 2

MAY 18, 1997

A.M.	latitude N 88° 20.644'	longitude W 75° 16.154'
P.M.	latitude N 88° 28.545'	longitude W 74° 49.071'
Distance traveled: 9 nm		Total nm from Ward Hunt: 324 nm
Hours traveled: 9 hrs.		Total nm to North Pole: 92 nm
Total hours traveled: 412.5 hrs.		Temperature: A.M. -12° C P.M. -11° C

A.M.

Happy Birthday to me! I was born 46 years ago in Philadelphia, Pennsylvania, the first of four children to Bob and Edith McNair, who ten years later won the national whitewater canoe slalom championships. Paddling and outdoor recreation was their hobby, not their professional life. Dad was a Harvard engineering graduate working for Westinghouse and Mom was an occupational therapist working as a mother. Never in my wildest dreams (and I have always been a dreamer) did I imagine that I would be dancing on the polar ice!

P.M.

Today was a gloriously sunny day with bright blue skies but a dark depressing day for me. I skied with Caroline all morning and, for four hours, I tried diplomatically to listen to and deal with her negative baggage and verbal abuse. Her main issue was my sending all my slide film directly to Paul. My contract stated that I was to return my original film to the Women's Polar Relay with each team going back to Resolute. Copies were to be made and kept by the expedition. The originals were to be returned to me. I am restricted from using these slides for one year. (This is a common expedition photo agreement. It allows the expedition to sell articles and photos to help recover their cost.) Prior to leaving Resolute, I expressed my concerns to Pen that I was not convinced that they had a proper system in place to keep my slide film separated from all the other relay women's film. I was concerned that my slides would get lost or misplaced. Pen agreed and gave me permission to send my film to Paul and have Paul make copies for the expedition. When I explained this to Caroline, she screeched back: "You are lying, you are lying." She continued to accuse me of placing the expedition in financial risk because she could not sell stories to the media without my pictures. I took a deep breath and calmly explained again, and again, and again. It was obvious that Pen had not told her about our agreement. Pen is an easy-going fellow who dislikes dealing with prickly situations; which is probably why he agreed to let me send my film to Paul in the first place and probably why he did not confess this to Caroline, knowing that it would bring her wrath on his head. For the last four changeovers, I have sent my film to Paul and no one mentioned that it was a problem⁶. I definitely feel I have been set up by Pen and used as a scapegoat. Why didn't they deal with this in Resolute before Caroline came on the ice? They knew how Caroline felt: Michael had warned me in his changeover note that "Caroline has a bee in her bonnet. Be careful."

Caroline also accused me of not pulling my fair share of the weight during the expedition. I explained to her that at times, when I was leading and navigating, my pulk was lighter. At other times it was heavier. I told her that my pulk weight varied according to my responsibilities on the ice and the energy of the individuals in the group. I also reminded her that we had discussed this issue with her and Pen back in January during their visit to Iqaluit. In order to ensure that Denise and I didn't burn out in the long run, we had agreed that the two leaders would carry less weight than the relay women, especially during the few days prior to changeovers. We wanted to ensure that Denise and I would be strong for the fresh group coming onto the ice. But Caroline did not want to hear what I had to say. She just kept accusing me of turning the expedition into: "helping Matty and Denise get to the North Pole." Where is this nonsense coming from? I don't understand Caroline. I feel she is blaming me for the failure of the expedition. Failure!!??? We are in striking distance of the Geographic North Pole. I don't think she wants to give Denise and me any credit for successfully and safely leading this expedition to this point and on to the Pole. On the other hand, maybe she does understand and she feels the need to crush me so she can be the "leader" and receive all the glory and honor. Anyway, I hope this outpouring of negative energy will allow her to focus her energy in a more positive direction.

By afternoon we came to a large open lead running east-west. Denise, with her eagle eyes, suggested that we turn west, so west it was. Soon our path was blocked by a secondary lead branching off the main lead, forcing us to detour southeast. Ironically, this forced us back to where we had stopped for our last break. While the group took a break, Denise and I scouted ahead. We came back with the news that there was a bridge of ice blocks not far ahead. I led across. At the far end of the ice bridge, I had to jump over a one-meter crack onto the bank. After I took the leap, Caroline followed. When she pushed off, an ice chunk broke free. This meant that those who followed had to use the free-floating ice chunk as a stepping stone. Pom was next. As she started to step over, she hesitated and the floater tipped. She made a desperate lunge for the shore. Caroline grabbed Pom and heaved her up out of the water with a powerful jerk. Unfortunately, the rescue slammed Pom's shoulder into a block of ice, momentarily dislocating her shoulder. We all held our breath, shocked by the sudden turn of events. Was she okay? Would we have to evacuate her? After a few moments, Pom composed herself and announced that she was OK, "only wet on the outside." Her shoulder was in pain but she thought that she could carry on. I recommended that she use an arm sling to give her shoulder a rest but she declined the offer.

---

6 Sending my slide film to Iqaluit was a stroke of luck. Unknown to me traveling on the ice, Pen threatened to withhold final payments to NorthWinds ($17,000 for guide & administrative fees and a $7,000 balance on equipment purchases). Paul decided to hold all of my slide film and use it as a bargaining tool for payment. Money owed to NorthWinds was finally cleared in November '97, 6 months overdue. Copies of my slides were sent to The Polar Travel Company immediately after we were paid in full.

As we looked after Pom, the crack widened, making the jump too risky. Denise, Lucy and Zoë continued along the far bank while Pom, Caroline and I skied the other bank.

We skied nearly an hour in a south-easterly direction along the lead before it narrowed enough to cross. We had circled around so far east that it now made more sense for Caroline, Pom and me to cross back. In the last two hours we had made a complete circle and accomplished negative nautical miles north. Oh well, so it goes, the Zen of Polar ice travel. It was nearly an hour before we found another place to attempt a crossing. More than halfway across, we came to a section of moving ice. A four-centimeter slab of ice from the north was rafting and pushing across the thicker eight-centimeter ice that we were on. It was fascinating to watch. I made ski tracks along the edge of the advancing slab of ice, then backed up to watch the ice crawl silently over my ski tracks. As the ice advanced, it plowed little piles of snow. It reminded me of a wave climbing up a sandy beach and pushing ahead a froth of bubbles.

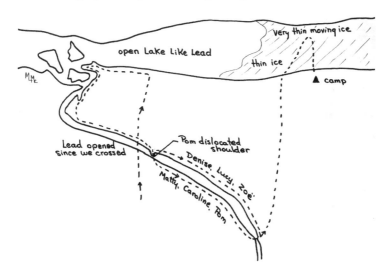

Blocked by this zone of thin ice, it was necessary to loop back and make camp on the south shore in hope of a change for tomorrow. We had skied nine hours, and even with all the back-tracking we knocked off another nine nautical miles. So far Team Echo is keeping up a good pace. Denise believes they can keep it up; I think that at this pace they will burn out.

Day 67 Echo Day 3

MAY 19, 1997

A.M.	latitude N 88° 29.234'	longitude W 74° 57.619'
P.M.	latitude N 88° 40.913'	longitude W 75° 21.656'
Distance traveled: 12.5 nm		Total nm from Ward Hunt: 336.5 nm
Hours traveled: 10 hrs.		Total nm to North Pole: 79.5 nm
Total hours traveled: 422.5 hrs.		Temperature: A.M. -8° C P.M. -8° C

This morning was overcast, with temperatures of -5° C and poor visibility. Over breakfast the group told Denise and me that they wanted to get to the Pole as quickly as possible. They declared, "We want to get to the Pole fast; we hate camping!" How strange: why are they doing this?

We had no trouble crossing the lead this morning. While we slept, Sedna had silently rearranged the ice so that this morning's lead no longer resembled the same lead that forced us to turn back yesterday afternoon. Beyond the lead the ice was generally flat with the occasional ice rubble. We hauled for ten hours, and with only two ski binding repairs to attend to, we recorded a 12.5 nautical mile gain on the Pole! The group comments on the day were, "So happy" and "Fucking excellent." I recorded these quotes under Group Morale in the Captain's Log.

In a very aggressive tone, Zoë confronted me as to why I always filled out the Captain's Log instead of having one of the relay members do it. I took a deep breath and quickly thought of a proper way to give her my answer, recognizing that she was looking for a confrontation. "Zoë, it is my responsibility, as leader, to keep track of our location, weather, ice conditions, group morale, etc. This is the expedition's official record. Pen and I agreed that I would be ultimately responsible and accountable for its contents and that I should fill out this Log. If there was ever a serious accident, this log would be submitted to the authorities. You are welcome to read this log, and copy any information you wish to add to your personal journal or to the group journal." I handed her the Captain's Log for her to look through and that was the end of this issue.

I have incubated another "Matty's Sense of Ice" theory: my accumulating experience is concluding that newly formed ice is stronger than refrozen chunks of older ice bonded together by thicker new ice. The new ice that forms over an expanse of open water, like a thin rubbery skin, is stronger because of its uniform elastic properties. Chunks of ice, on the other hand, re-frozen together with new ice, are more likely to give way under our weight. When we step on these blocks of inflexible ice, the bond snaps between the old ice chunks and the new ice. It's easy to fall into the illusion that it is safer to step across a lead on these ice blocks bonded by eight centimeters of new ice than to ski over a six-centimeter thick skin of new ice. The uniform flexibility of the new ice is one factor; the other is that on skis, our weight is more evenly distributed on flat new ice than when skiing or stepping on ice blocks. Experience is the greatest teacher.

Day 68 Echo Day 4

MAY 20, 1997

A.M.   latitude N 88° 41.049'   longitude W 75° 18.554'
P.M.   latitude N 88° 53.091'   longitude W 75° 31.011'
Distance traveled: 12.3 nm   Total nm from Ward Hunt: 349 nm
Hours traveled: 11 hrs.   Total nm to North Pole: 67.2 nm
Total hours traveled: 433.5 hrs.   Temperature: A.M. -5° C P.M. -8° C

Another endless day; my pulk was very heavy and was grinding me down. I feel I have to prove to Caroline that I can pull a heavy pulk. She does not accept that as leaders, Denise and I have added responsibilities. We often must zip ahead to shoot bearings or to scout routes over pressure ridges and around leads. As leader, I should be able to carry a lighter pulk and not feel guilty about it.

I skied with Denise in the afternoon and had a good cry. My first of the trip. The tension with Caroline is wearing on me. There is absolutely no recognition of or appreciation for the hard work Denise and I have contributed to this expedition. She does not acknowledge that under my leadership we are now 67 nautical miles from the North Pole and the chance of success is very high. She does not recognize that, on my own time, I - not Pen - purchased $75,000 worth of food, equipment and clothing for this expedition. I should point out to her that my contract ended on May 17 and Denise and I are no longer being paid.

This journal is becoming my "bitch and moan" confessional. I am with these women 24 hours a day and I need a place to off-load my negative feelings so I can maintain an upbeat and professional attitude towards my clients.

On our evening sched call, Pen told us that the Dutch were being picked up at the North Pole tomorrow. He went on to say that in the last couple of days the Dutch team had encountered countless open leads; five times in one day they had to use their larger pulk as a boat to ferry across open leads. Pen informed me that he had made arrangements to have First Air drop off a "boat" on their way to pick up the Dutch. If the plane could land, we would have the choice of using a rubber raft or a borrowed spare pulk (a large one) from the Dutch expedition. If the plane could not land they would drop the raft. I asked for a description and weight of the raft: "It's an old patched up raft weighing about 14 kilograms. I will send you a repair kit. Take the pump on long crossings as the raft may deflate some." Oh wow! Why didn't Pen consult with me? Again, decisions affecting travel on the ice are being made without any consultation with or input from me. I am on the ice and can best evaluate the situation. If I thought I needed a boat I would have requested that we borrow one from NorthWinds (we have light weight inflatable canoes that roll up to be the size of a large sleeping bag) or use Will Steger's canoes at Ward Hunt Island.

Day 69 Echo Day 5

MAY 21, 1997

A.M.   latitude N 88° 53.172'   longitude W 75° 08.488'
P.M.   latitude N 89° 02.136'   longitude W 72° 47.222'
Distance traveled: 9 nm   Total nm from Ward Hunt: 358 nm
Hours traveled: 11 hrs.   Total nm to North Pole: 58.2 nm
Total hours traveled: 444.5 hrs.   Temperature: A.M. -8° C P.M. -5° C

Another long day in the life of the Women's Polar Relay. Boredom was kept at bay by the need to locate a runway for the boat drop off. To speed up the group pace, I took the lead, dashing ahead to shoot bearings and to find routes through ice rubble and small leads before the group caught up to me. An excellent work-out with my heavy pulk.

At 11:30 a.m., 1:30 p.m. and 2:30 p.m. we halted to set up the radio to relay weather reports directly to the pilots en route to pick up the Dutch. It seemed that the Dutch radio was low on batteries and the pilots needed weather updates from us. Doug, the First Air pilot emphasized the need to locate a landing strip since he thought the raft was, "too large to push out the door of the plane." Unfortunately, even pushing at a fast pace we were unable to locate a runway by the time Doug spotted us at 2:45 p.m. We waited by the radio as the plane circled north, south, east and west searching for a landing strip. We waited and watched and shouted to the wind, "Come on, Doug, bring it down, you can do it, don't give up, go north, go north." We had nearly given up hope when the plane set down two nautical miles to the north-northeast of us.

Off we dashed like race horses at a Kentucky Derby, motivated by contact from the civilized world. When we neared the plane, the pilots, Doug and Luke, walked out to greet us. They shook our hands and congratulated us. From the respect that they extended to us, I knew they thought we were going to succeed.

I was surprised by the enormous bundle by the plane. The raft must have weighed between 30 and 35 kilograms and was larger than our pulks! I couldn't believe Pen had sent this to us. There was no question in my mind that the raft was totally inappropriate. It would slow us down more than skiing around large leads. I decided that we would take the Dutch pulk instead and use it as a boat if we needed to. (It was made of Kevlar, which is stronger and lighter than fiberglass, was three meters long, with high 50-centimeter sides, and weighed about 11 kilograms.)

My own pulk, having gone the entire distance from Ward Hunt, was in the worst condition so I sent it back and loaded my gear into the Dutch pulk. Pen had sent in a full fiberglass repair kit. I immediately put this into the pile of stuff to return to Resolute. Caroline confronted me as to why I did not want to bring this repair kit. She was not satisfied by a short explanation, so I had to give her my full résumé: I was a white-water paddler, had built 13 boats myself, taught courses on building fiberglass kayaks and worked with polyester, epoxy and vinylester resins. I explained that if the resin froze it would be useless and, even if we could keep it from freezing, to get the resin to cure would require heating the tent to a dry 25° C for two to three hours. I explained that if small cracks developed in the bottom of the pulk, they would not damage the structural integrity of the pulk and could be patched easily with duct tape.

Doug and Luke were so kind, and patiently waited while I talked to Caroline. She finally let go of the issue. The pilots stood by the plane for photos, insisted that we accept their lunch of two oranges, grapes and muffins and Doug kept thanking us—for what I don't know. "No, no," I responded, "it's me that thanks you for looking so hard for a runway and landing so that we could pick up the pulk and not have to drag that raft!"

I sense a change in attitude from First Air and the residents of Resolute about our expedition. As we inch towards the Pole, we have gained their respect. Earlier, I am sure that they were laughing behind our backs and placing bets that these inexperienced British women, who could hardly ski, would never succeed. Which reminds me, Karen Bradburn (Team Bravo) said that her brother had placed a £1,000 bet, at great odds, that the Women's Polar Relay would make it to the Pole!

The rest of the day was a plod. With all the stops to set up the radio and the time spent at the plane, we only managed nine nautical miles in 11 hours. We have now crossed the 89th degree of latitude, which leaves one degree to go! The end is in sight. (One degree = 60 nautical miles or about 120 kilometers.)

Day 70 Echo Day 6

MAY 22, 1997

A.M.	latitude N 89° 01.536'	longitude W 72° 33.226'
P.M.	latitude N 89° 11.226'	longitude W 74° 25.591'
Distance traveled: 9 nm		Total nm from Ward Hunt: 367 nm
Hours traveled: 10 hrs.		Total nm to North Pole: 49 nm
Total hours traveled: 454.5 hrs.		Temperature: A.M. -3° C P.M. -10° C

We were slow getting off this morning. The group had lost its zip and drive. I must admit that Team Echo started off their relay leg at a fast pace and kept it up longer than I expected. But now we are down to a slow plodding pace. I don't think the relay women are aware of how much speed they have lost, as perhaps their effort seems the same to them.

The pace is frustrating for Denise and me. With our goal so close we want to make a mad dash for the Pole and so we keep taking on more weight in our pulks. Although this team prides themselves on their supportive team work, rarely have I seen them go out of their way to physically help each other over obstacles. Their support consists of shouting verbal encouragement. It is Denise and I that unclip from our pulks and return to help when crossing pressure ridges.

This afternoon the right binding tore off Caroline's ski. Upon closer inspection I discovered that the screw inserts had not been installed! I tried the old trick of stuffing steel wool into the screw holes. That lasted for an hour. Next option was to epoxy the screws in.

The group was quick to discount my method for repairing the binding: "No, the epoxy makes its own heat; it'll set up even when it's cold...," they insisted. Though I knew this was bullshit, the experiential educator in me stepped back to let them discover the truth for themselves. They were in a great hurry to stuff the epoxy into the screw holes and screw down the binding before it set up. I took a lighter and heated half of the leftover epoxy. It set up in two minutes. This finally convinced the group that we needed to put a stove under the ski. But Lucy kept testing the glue by turning the screws and so broke any bond that was forming. Folks were getting cold and impatient. Caroline declared that she would walk so that we could carry on. I strapped her skis onto my pulk with a warm water bottle wrapped around the epoxied screw.

So we limped forward, Caroline stumbling into hidden cracks and Pom using one ski pole, with the arm of her injured shoulder held across her chest. I offered my skis to Caroline but she preferred walking at this point. Later Denise offered her skis and she accepted.

We saw two seals! One was basking on the ice and slipped back in the water when she heard us; the second popped his head up in a lead to check us out.

This evening Caroline told me that during their training in Resolute they were able to ski ten nautical miles in six hours. Yet today it took us ten hours to cover nine nautical miles. They were surprised that they are not leaping over the miles as they had expected to. This over-estimation of miles, based on training performance, is a mistake commonly made by many expeditions. I remember training dogs for our dog sledding expedition around Baffin Island. During training, the dogs could easily cover 100 kilometers a day! Yet on the expedition it was hard to average even 50 kilometers a day. It's one of those unexplained mysteries of arctic travel.

The epoxy never set up on Caroline's ski binding. I solved the problem by remounting the binding with new screw holes, three centimeters forward of the stripped-out holes. I don't know why this simple solution eluded me earlier. Without screw inserts the binding may pull out again, so Caro will use my skis.

Day 71 Echo Day 7

MAY 23, 1997

A.M.   latitude N 89° 10.539'   longitude W 73° 22.122'
P.M.   latitude N 89° 19.284'   longitude W 72° 33.817'
Distance traveled: 9 nm   Total nm from Ward Hunt: 376 nm
Hours traveled: 11.5 hrs.   Total nm to North Pole: 40.9 nm
Total hours traveled: 466 hrs.   Temperature: A.M. -10° C P.M. -10° C

We only accomplished nine nautical miles in 11.5 hours. I say only because at this point we should be traveling one nautical mile an hour. With warmer temperatures it is much easier to complete tasks such as putting on and taking off skis, going for a pee and setting up and taking down camp. Our skis and pulks now glide and the ice is also flatter and there are fewer pressure ridges. All good conditions for efficient travel, yet the group can't push much more than what we did today.

We traveled around numerous small open leads and over a few large leads covered with thin ice. Nearly across one of these newly refrozen leads, I came to a band of ice so thin that my ski pole punched through. When I announced that we would have to turn back and find another route, there was a lot of grumbling. Caroline said, "Why don't you try it? What if we skied fast; we should be able to get across." No one likes to turn back, least of all me. But I did not appreciate the pressure from the group to take such a stupid risk.

Over the last few weeks, we have seen piles of oily ice blocks. I wonder where they come from. The black oil smudges spoil this pristine wilderness, untouched by the soiled hands of humankind. In one fantasy, I have us discovering and exposing to the world that a Russian oil tanker, secretly attempting to push through the polar ice, was ripped open by an iceberg, spilling millions of gallons of oil.

Tonight is the third night in a row that the dinner was burnt by neglect. A burnt dinner at home is no big deal—you go to the freezer and dig out another meal or order out for a pizza. Up here every gram of food is essential. If we are unable to consume a burnt dinner, we will not be consuming our required 4,500 daily calories. Three burnt dinners is not the end of the world, but it adds up and could start an avalanche of mishaps in this unforgiving environment. I call it the Domino Effect. For example, you go to bed without the calories of a good dinner to burn and so have a cold, sleepless night (domino #1). The next day you are feeling lethargic and don't bother to have a second hot drink after breakfast (domino #2). As dehydration sets in, your head starts to ache and you are unwilling to eat more that a few bites of food at each break (domino #3). As your energy level declines, you fall more often, wasting more energy (domino #4). Your morale starts to slide (domino #5). By the end of the day you are running on empty, without any reserves to fall back on (domino #6). All it takes now is one small minor incident to topple the dominos. You fail to change your damp mitts and frostbite your fingers, or you fall through the ice and are unable to ward off hypothermia. For me, a burnt dinner is two dominoes: decreased calories and low morale.

Lucy was not feeling well today (another domino). She claimed to have had chills and fever all day. However, she kept up a good pace and did not slow the group down. Lucy is a small woman but she can haul her own weight without grumbling.

What has slowed us down the last few days are:

1. this group has lost its zip and drive.

2. these women do not understand the glide concept in cross-country skiing.

3. they are unwilling to have Denise and me teach them skiing techniques.

I cringe every time they pull out the video camera to film each other skiing. Most walk upright and some even lift their ski tips with every step, making herringbone tracks. Others ski with elbows bent, using their poles like walking canes. In part, the women do not see the point in learning to glide because Pen told them they would be walking and that skiing skills were unnecessary. The first group, Team Alfa, did walk most of the time, on hard-packed hummocks. But since Alfa, the snow has been too soft and the ice too thin to walk. Somewhere I recall reading that if Scott, on his return from the South Pole, had traveled another 125 meters a day, he would have made "One Ton Depot" and he and his companions would not have perished. I am convinced that this could have been achieved without expending more energy if one had basic ski technique.

$\mathcal{D}ay$ 72 $\mathcal{E}cho$ $\mathcal{D}ay$ 8

MAY 24, 1997

A.M.   latitude N 89° 18.545'   longitude W 70° 47.856'
P.M.   latitude N 89° 28.544'   longitude W 75° 12.729'
Distance traveled: 9.3 nm   Total nm from Ward Hunt: 385.3 nm
Hours traveled: 10.5 hrs.   Total nm to North Pole: 31.6 nm
Total hours traveled: 476.5 hrs.   Temperature: A.M. -11° C P.M. -10° C

This morning when I stepped out of the tent, the scene looked exactly the same as it did last night: a pressure ridge of ice blocks behind the tent, a weathered ice hummock to the right, and endless ice rubble to the north. But it is an illusion. I am not at the same location on the planet this morning as when I went into the tent last night. During the night we drifted 2° E and 1' S. This is a difficult concept to contemplate and understand. We must always remember that we are traveling on a floating island of ice.

Another overcast and gloomy day. To pick up the pace I took the lead with Denise's lighter pulk. I was able to zip ahead to scout the easiest routes. I enjoyed the problem-solving challenges of leading: to go right over a narrow ice bridge or left around the black ice, to cross where the ice has rafted or travel on the newly formed smooth ice. I led all day and we made nine nautical miles north in 10.5 hours. Miles and hours seem to be my life. Miles represent the inches we have gained towards our goal. Hours equal the amount of energy that the miles have cost us. The 476.5 hours that I've been hauling pulks have toughened up my muscles but are grinding me down in other ways. My feet are giving out. I suspect my arches are falling since they have been sending me distress signals for weeks. My big toes have been numb and without feeling for two weeks now. My toes have never been cold, so I assume it's from slamming my foot forward into the toe of the boot for 72 days.

Yesterday Lucy was not feeling well. Today Zoë had a downer day. She made us laugh when she said tonight, "I got the wrong body on today, hope to have a better one tomorrow." It's 1:00 a.m. I'm not tired, so while snores resound around me, I'm writing in bed.

Day 73 Echo Day 9

MAY 25, 1997

A.M.   latitude N 89° 28.688'   longitude W 72° 16.825'
P.M.   latitude N 89° 44.461'   longitude W 73° 04.416'
Distance traveled: 16 nm   Total nm from Ward Hunt: 401.3 nm
Hours traveled: 11 hrs.   Total nm to North Pole: 15.6 nm
Total hours traveled: 487.5 hrs.   Temperature: A.M. -8° C P.M. -7° C

What an amazing day it was. The conditions have finally changed to nearly flat!! We skied 11 hours and covered a record 16 nautical miles north!! Wow! We did not encounter any open leads but only a few small frozen ones. It was as if we had moved back into winter with all the leads frozen over. But the temperatures were only -7° C. Skiing was a pleasure on a hard wind-packed base covered with one centimeter of light powder snow. I could even get a few centimeters of glide while hauling my pulk and with my ski skins on.

We are all very tired but pleased and encouraged by our incredible progress. Tomorrow is Denise's birthday. We will do our utmost to reach the Pole for her birthday. The end is in sight. I can't believe we are almost there.

Day 74 Echo Day 10

MAY 26, 1997

A.M.   latitude N 89° 45.258'   longitude W 67° 20.952'
P.M.   latitude N 89° 59.999'   longitude W 74°
Distance traveled: 15 nm   Total nm from Ward Hunt: 416 nm
Hours traveled: 12 hrs.   Total nm to North Pole: 0 nm
Total hours traveled: 499.5 hrs.   Temperature: A.M. -8° C P.M. -5° C

A.M.

This, I hope, will be our big day to reach the Pole. If we do, it will be a very special 31st birthday for Denise. Denise will become the first Canadian woman to reach the North Pole. (Although I have married a French Canadian and have made my home in Canada for nearly 20 years, I am a U.S. citizen.)

Today, both Denise and I will carry our GPS next to our bodies in order to keep the batteries warm. This will allow us to check our location and readjust the magnetic declination on our compasses throughout the day. As we get closer to our goal, precision navigation will become critical.

P.M.

Over the course of the day, I kept an accurate record of our progress towards our long dreamed-of, long worked-for goal:

	Latitude	Longitude	Mag. Declin.	Miles to NP
Camp #73	89° 45.258'	67° 20.952'	101° W	15.6
1:00 P.M.	89° 47.916'	64° 39.986'	93° W	12.1
2:30 P.M.	89° 50.185'	66° 03.501'	95° W	9.8
3:45 P.M.	89° 52.663'	65° 35.241'	94° W	7.3
5:00 P.M.	89° 54.623'	64° 01.854'	93° W	5.2
7:00 P.M.	89° 56.999'	66° 13.799'	69° W	3.3

At 9:00 p.m. I pulled out my GPS so I could navigate while I skied. It indicated that we were 1.3 nautical miles from the Pole and that the Pole was now to the east (right) of us. I checked in with Denise, who was skiing at the back and also checking our course with her GPS. According to her observations, the miles were still decreasing and she recommended that we continue on our present compass bearing. On I went, following my compass bearing. I crossed over a pressure ridge and, while I waited for the group on the other side of the ridge, I continued to walk in the direction my compass indicated and held my GPS in my hand. I entered North Pole in the "Go To" display. As I walked, the GPS obtained readings from satellites and recalculated my present location, indicating the direction of travel that I needed to go to reach my requested destination. As I walked, the GPS indicated that the North Pole was ninety degrees to my right (east). As I continued to walk on my compass bearing, the distance to the North Pole increased. Denise joined me at this point. We compared our GPS readings and agreed that the North Pole was .5 nautical miles to the east. We soon came onto a large flat pan of multi-year ice. I informed the group that we were near the Pole. Caroline pulled out her British flag and requested that we line up, six abreast. Forward we marched. "Stop," commanded Caroline, "We need the video camera." She told Denise and me to remove our "other" clothing and put on the sponsored clothing. We continued our march while Denise and I called out the GPS readings: ".3" ".2" ".1" ".2" ".3". At this point Denise and I unclipped from our pulks and walked back to where the GPS indicated ".1". From this point, we started a grid pattern. While Team Echo stood with British flag poised, ready to be planted at the exact North Pole, Denise and I walked around, calling out, "I've got .03," "I've got .01!"

When the GPS read: 89 59.999' (note: a GPS cannot read 90° 000'), Denise made a small pile of snow and I announced, "At this moment in time, this is the Geographic North Pole."

It was 10:45 p.m. on May 26, 1997. The Women's Polar Relay expedition had reached its goal and became the first women's expedition to reach the Geographic North Pole.

Team Echo now moved into position. Denise and I were asked to "step out of the picture" and take photographs and video their North Pole speeches. They started with naming the members of each team:

Team Alfa:	**Team Bravo:**	
Ann Daniels	Rose Agnew	
Claire Fletcher	Karen Bradburn	
Sue Fullilove	Catherine Clubb	
Jan McCormac	Emma Scott	

Team Charlie:	**Team Delta:**	**Team Echo:**
Lynne Clarke	Andre Chadwick	Caroline Hamilton
Paula Power	Rosie Stancer	Zoë Hudson
Susan Riches	Sarah Jones	Pom Oliver
Victoria Riches	Juliette May	Lucy Roberts

They thanked the list of sponsors that had helped them with donations of money and goods, the support team in Resolute, family and friends. They failed to mention Denise and me. How very British. Historically Brits rarely mentioned the Sherpas that hauled them up the Himalayas or the Inuit that sledded them across the Arctic. To me it's not a big deal anymore: it's their dream, their money and so it's their expedition. They get the recognition and glory, I got the opportunity to lead this expedition, to travel for 74 days on the Polar sea and I got paid. (Money is not a motivator in my life, but it would be unfair not to admit that I was paid well.)

Team Echo ended their North Pole ceremony with "God Save the Queen," their voices slowly swallowed by the great white vastness. The exhilaration of reaching the Pole quickly faded as hunger, cold and exhaustion claimed their attention. We'd skied 15 nautical miles in 12 hours. I suggested that we camp "at the North Pole," in the lee of a nearby pressure ridge. While they proceeded to set up the tent, Denise and I took our own North Pole photos.

At first, standing on the North Pole was not as exhilarating as reaching the top of a high mountain. When I climb a mountain, there is a building sense of suspense as the final summit comes into view. When I take that final step, I get an "On Top of the World" thrill. The whole world falls away and I am rewarded with a 360° panoramic view. I am above the clouds, above earthly cares. I am in heaven.

The North Pole is not a geographically fixed place that you can claim with your country's flag. There is no red and white pole with a silver sphere to mark the spot, such as there is at the South Pole. The Geographic North Pole is an invented concept, where all of the lines of longitude meet. It takes imagination to find the magic.

As Denise and I took pictures, I was slowly overwhelmed with an amazing feeling: I was standing on the top of the world. Here I could spin through all the time zones in the world! So what time was it, I wondered? If I spinned around the Pole, clockwise, maybe I could turn time backwards and become younger. (I tried but got dizzy.)

Another odd realization was that no matter which way I turned I was facing South. North, east and west no longer existed. Every day, all year round, the winds always came from the south, blew over the pole and passed on southwards. Fixed directly above me, obscured by the sunlit atmosphere, was the North Star. In the dead of winter, all the illuminated heavenly bodies, stars, constellations, planets and nebulae, whirled around the North Star, never rising or setting below the horizon.

Wow, I am on top of the world—both literally and figuratively! Reaching the Geographic North Pole is my Everest.

I can go no further north. I have accomplished my job of leading five teams of four women safely to the North Pole. I can now turn south, home to Paul, Sarah and Eric. I wonder how to express to them what this experience has been for me. How will I explain the magic of the pastel arctic light on the sculptured waves of sastrugis, the pressure ridges of blue ice blocks and the fragile beauty of the ice crystals growing on new ice? It has been a long journey. The achievement of reaching the North Pole fulfills me for now, but what I will carry in my heart forever is this extraordinary journey over the polar ice that I shared with my friend Denise and these twenty wonderful women.

The ice and moonlit nights, with all their yearning,
seemed like a far off dream from another world-
a dream that has come and passed away.
But what would life be worth without its dreams?

Fridtjof Nansen, Farthest North

Afterword

June 2

FLYING SOUTH IN THE TWIN OTTER

As the plane droned south I gazed out the window. Below was a network of black jagged patterns cutting through the ice. Either the ice had opened considerably in the last week or we were lucky and had traveled along a corridor of solid ice. Under an endless dome of blue sky it all looked so peaceful and serene from up here, smooth and white with an overlay of tiny wrinkles. Warm sunlight sparkled and danced along the leads of open water.

Not all had gone as planned. We reached the Geographic North Pole on May 26, 1997. We set up camp, sent an Argos message (proof to the world of our location), and strung up the radio wires to share the good news with the support team in Resolute. No answer. After numerous attempts there was still no answer. Eventually,

First Air came on to inform us that the entire support team had flown to Eureka and were planning to fly to the Pole for our pick up. We proceeded to celebrate Denise's birthday. We hung balloons on the drying lines around the top of the tent, sang happy birthday and passed around a small bag of candy that I had hoarded. At 2:00 a.m. we collapsed into bed and dreamed of the plane arriving the next morning.

We woke to the dismal reality of low overcast skies. For the next six days we waited for the plane. The pan of ice that we were camped on drifted over the Pole towards Siberia and spiraled counter-clockwise around the Pole. We had arrived at the Pole with four days of food left. After two days we went on half rations and then on quarter rations. Days and nights became a gray blur as Denise and I called in weather updates every two hours to First Air in Resolute. Since our support team was in Eureka, we were left with no one to communicate with. I worried that family and friends, unable to get news of us, would become anxious.

To ration fuel, we only fired up the stoves to cook and melt snow for hot drinks. To keep warm, I went for walks. Dizzy from lack of food, I often sat, listening to the wind blowing snow over the ice. Denise kept herself amused by building a row of Inuksuks (Inuit cairns, "in the like-ness of a man"), and I worked on a four-meter snow sculpture of Sedna. In the tent I spent most of my time in my sleeping bag, sliding between dreams and daydreams, watching the mitts bounce on the drying lines as the wind pounded on the tent.

Inuksuk
Snow Sculptures
made by Denise at the North Pole

After my 80 days on the ice, the Twin Otter finally arrived to lift us off the loneliest place on earth. In six days we had drifted 15 nautical miles from the North Pole.

June 10

2 WEEKS LATER

I expected to return home the same person that I was before the expedition. It was difficult for me to grapple with the fact that I was not and could not be. I had journeyed to the North Pole, and that journey had marked me in ways too subtle to explain.

For 80 days I carried the illusion that when I came home, everything would continue as before. And yet after two weeks at home, I still find myself floating, lost in space, caught in a time warp. I am unable to sleep more than five to six hours a night. Denise, in Whitehorse (Yukon), is experiencing much the same. During the last four months, my attention and focus was to travel north. I suddenly find myself lost without any immediate and tangible goal. I've been gone for so long that I often feel I've lost my place in my family and our company, NorthWinds. I often feel I'm not needed. Eric has become a teenager and is solving math problems that leave my head spinning (Paul and I have been homeschooling Eric for three years). Sarah thinks that she is a teenager (age 11) and keeps the stereo blasting with groups that I've never heard of like Aqua, Hanson Boys and Spice Girls. Paul has managed NorthWinds on his own for the last five months and the summer programs are all planned and ready. And only the older dogs remember me.

Scotty, Nobu and Acchan (Polar Free Expedition) came over for dinner. They reached the Pole the day before we were lifted off. It was great comparing notes about the ice and sharing feelings on our success.

July

ONE MONTH LATER

Paul took Sarah and Eric south so they can spend three weeks with grand-maman, his mother, in northern Ontario. I drift aimlessly around the house watering plants, catching up on correspondence and sorting through slides of the expedition. I spend time in the dog yard, caring for and feeding our 28 sled dogs and four puppies.

I started to transfer my journal onto the computer. Looking at pictures and working with my journal is good therapy as it allows me to review the journey. There are many feelings that I had pushed aside that I need to come to terms with.

My big toes are still numb from the continuous slamming into the front of my boots. My feet still hurt. The left foot more than the right. The worst is in the morning when I first put my full weight on them. I am seeing a Shiatsu therapist.

October

FIVE MONTHS LATER

Denise and I have been in constant contact. She's in Saskatoon taking a ceramics course. She misses being up in the Arctic and working with sled dogs. I assured her that if NorthWinds has another North Pole trip I will ask her to co-lead it with me. I hope to have her come up this winter and work NorthWinds programs in south Baffin.

And myself? The empty, lost, drifting feelings have faded. Over the summer, in between leading NorthWinds adventures on the Soper River, I worked on my journal and put together a slide show. This has helped me to work through my post-expedition depressions. I don't understand these feelings. After the four-month Baffin Island Expedition, I was exuberant and full of zest. Yet, only now am I feeling buoyed up by the success of what I achieved.

March

TEN MONTHS LATER

Paul and I traveled to London, England, for a travel show in early March. I took the opportunity to get together with Victoria, Rose, Andre and Caroline in an English pub for a few beers.

Victoria (Team Charlie) picked me up at my hotel. On the way to the pub, she confided that she and Lucy (Team Echo) were planning an expedition from Ward Hunt Island to the North Pole for 1999. They wanted to be the first British women to do the entire trek. Victoria went on to say that she and Sue, her mother, had been giving slide shows on their experiences and were working on a book titled, Frigid Women. Victoria explained, "There is no sex in the book so we thought we'd sell it in the title."

At the pub were Rose (Team Bravo) and her husband. Andre (Team Delta) arrived in a black leather jacket with a motor cycle helmet under her arm. She announced that she was getting married! A little later Caroline joined us. She was in a jolly mood, alluding to other "plans" and maybe a book.

Jan McCormac was unable to come, but I had a wonderful talk with her on the telephone and she filled me in on some of the other relay women. Emma (Team Bravo) was in school finishing her degree in recreation. Sarah (Team Delta) had changed jobs. Juliette (Team Delta) had ended her relationship and was now involved with Nobby (from the support team).

I also had a long telephone conversation with Ann (Team Alpha), the mother of the triplets. Her husband was asking for a divorce. I asked her if this was a repercussion from the expedition. She said no. When we talked again the next day, she said yes the expedition had contributed to the divorce.

Me. Well I'm feeling great. I am more like the old me again, full of energy and bounce. The old "Tigger" I once was. My life is in perspective, buoyed up by the success of our North Pole Adventure.

People are always asking me what's next, what other adventures. Spend time with Paul, of course, and with Eric and Sarah before the children leave home to follow their own adventures.

And, I've decided to write a book. . .

Appendix 1

NEWS RELEASE   MAY 27, 1997

Matty McNair leads the first
All Women Expedition to the North Pole

All Women Expedition Reaches the North Pole

Yesterday (May 26) at 22:45 central time, the Women's Polar Relay Expedition reached the North Pole. This is the first ever all women's expedition to successfully complete the entire journey from Ward Hunt Island (northern Ellesmere Island) to the North Pole. After 74 days of hard work, Matty and the women were ecstatic to reach the North Pole and contribute their remarkable achievement to polar history.

The first ever all women expedition to reach the North Pole

Polar exploration and expeditions has been dominated by male expeditions. A few women have reached the North Pole, but always as part of all male expeditions. The Women's Polar Relay Expedition becomes the first all women expedition to reach the North Pole. Also, Matty McNair and Denise Martin became the first two women to have ever traveled the entire distance from Ward Hunt Island to the North Pole without the aid of dogs or machines.

The first ever "guided" expedition from Ward Hunt Island to the North Pole

NorthWinds, owned and operated by Matty McNair and Paul Landry, were contracted to provide guiding services to the Women's Polar Relay Expedition. Matty assumed the responsibility of chief guide and Denise Martin was hired as assistant guide. Throughout the fall and early winter, Matty coordinated the selection, purchasing and testing of equipment, clothing and food for the expedition.

Through an intense selection process, twenty "ordinary women" from all walks of life were chosen to participate in the expedition. None of the women had previous winter or polar experience. After a 10 day training in Resolute Bay, groups of four women joined Matty and Denise on the Polar sea for a 15 day expedition before passing on the baton to the next team.

Not only did the women reach the North Pole, but they did it in style. Thanks to Matty's expert leadership, guidance and attention to details, none of the women suffered any frostbite or injuries. All the women returned healthy and strong.

The first Canadian woman to reach the North Pole

Denise Martin (assistant guide and NorthWinds staff) is the first Canadian woman to travel from Ward Hunt Island to the North Pole. A native of Saskatoon, Denise was recruited by NorthWinds because of her extensive winter experience, including 3 winters in Baffin Island working with NorthWinds, her strong determination and her physical strength. Denise reached the North Pole on her 31st birthday.

Appendix 2

PRE-EXPEDITION LETTER TO RELAY MEMBERS

January 27, 1997

Dear Relay Members,

We are about to embark on a historic event. The outcome will depend on how prepared we are and how well we meet the challenges the Arctic has to offer: extreme cold, raging storms, shifting ice packs, and endless pressure ridges.

The process of reaching the North Pole may be identified with a game of chess where all the moves, leading to a favorable outcome, have been thoroughly thought out in advance, long before the beginning of the game.

From the diary of Robert Peary

We are a well-supported team with the best-tested equipment, most up-to-date communication systems and a solid support team to back us up. The rest is up to us: to relay to the NORTH POLE. In preparation:

Physical Training:
We need to develop strength, flexibility and (if possible) cross-country skiing skills.

For Strength:
- pull 2 tires using ski poles to simulate skiing (if you are making 1 kph that's about the right amount of difficulty)
- bound up long sets of stairs or stadium steps
- walk with weights on ankles (skis + boots = 2.55 kg per foot!)
- lift weights to build upper body strength
- strengthen stomach muscles (to protect back)
- use a X-C pole exerciser (we gave Caroline an easy-to-make model)
- strengthen arches in feet with repeats of lifting up on toes (boots do not have arch supports)

For Flexibility:
- stretching, stretching, stretching
- yoga
- ballet, modern dance

For X-C Skiing:
- back-country skiing (off trail), classic track skiing, skate skiing, downhill skiing on X-C skis, telemark skiing
- downhill skiing: learn to move on big feet, fall down (on side, not face), get up on a slope, side step or herringbone uphill
- work out on a Nordic ski exercise machine
- watch videos of X-C skiing

Other Things You Can Do:
- Get used to sleeping on a hard surface in the confines of a tight sleeping bag. On expedition you will be sleeping with your water bottle, wet socks, batteries and anything else that must be dried or kept warm.
- Get used to the idea that we will not let you take your favorite toys: no pillows, no teddy bears, no walkman…We will be ruthless about extra weight!!!
- Hate that greasy head feeling? Start washing your hair less often. The less you wash your hair, the less oil your scalp will produce.
- If you have a hard-to-control menstrual cycle or don't want to bother with your period at -40° C, talk to your doctor. about going on a continuous cycle of the Pill.
- Working hard in an extremely dry cold climate leads to dehydration, which contributes significantly to hypothermia and frostbite. Start getting used to drinking four liters a day. Your drinks should be caffeine free to count as a hydrating source.
- Cut down significantly on caffeine intake. Caffeine is a diuretic, which means that it robs your body of vital fluids and in the Arctic contributes to dehydration.
- Try to put on a few extra pounds. Even consuming 5,000 calories a day, you will lose weight. The extra weight will ensure that your body can withstand the cold and you will shed that weight, plus more. (Matty lost 18 lbs. in 16 days on the Baffin Island Expedition when temperatures were -40° C and below.)
- Make a dental appointment if you have not seen a dentist recently.
- Do not get sick before coming to the Arctic. One little virus can devastate the entire team.

WE LOOK FORWARD TO SHARING A GREAT ARCTIC ADVENTURE WITH YOU!

Matty McNair and Denise Martin

Appendix 3

ORIGINAL AND ACTUAL ITINERARY

	Dates	Days on ice	Storm/ Change	Travel Days	Mileage per/day	Team Mileage	Point
Alfa Team #1							
–projected:	March 13–27	15	3	12	3.0	36	83°.45'
–actual:	March 14–30	17	5	12	4.6	56	
Changeover							
–projected:	March 28 @ 83° 45'						
–actual:	March 30 @ 84° 02'						
Bravo Team #2							
–projected:	March 27–April 9	14	3	11	5.0	55	84°.39'
–actual:	March 30–April 12	14	2	12	5.7	69	
Changeover							
-projected:	April 9 @ 84° 39'						
–actual:	April 12 @ 85° 10'						
Charlie Team #3							
–projected:	April 9–24	16	3	13	7	91	85°.46'
–actual:	April 12–28	17	3	14	5	70	
Changeover							
–projected:	April 24 @ 85° 46'						
–actual:	April 28 @ 86° 21'						
Delta Team #4							
–projected:	April 24–May 9	16	3	13	8.5	110.5	87°.20'
–actual:	April 28–May 17	19	4	15	7.3	110	
Changeover							
–projected:	May 9 @ 87° 20'						
–actual:	May 17 @ 88° 10'						
Echo Team #5							
–projected:	May 9–26	18	4	14	9	126	90°
–actual:	May 17–26	10	0	10	11	110	

–projected arrival at North Pole: May 26
–actual arrival at North Pole: May 26

Notes:
1.   Changeover days not included as part of travel days column.
2.   Team mileage is calculated by multiplying travel days with daily mileage.

Appendix 4

"ARGOS" DAILY POSITIONS

Date		Latitude	Distance Gained N.	Longitude	Evening Temperature °C	Argos Code *
Ward Hunt	Fri.	83,05		74,05		
March 14	Fri.	83,07	2	74,14	-39	0000
March 15	Sat.	83,10	3	74,03	-35	0000
March 16	Sun.	83,11	1	74,15	-34	0100
March 17	Mon.	83,14	3	74,20	-34	0000
March 18	Tues.	83,19	5	74,10	-30	0000
March 19	Wed.	83,25	6	74,14	-29	0000
March 20	Thurs.	83,30	5	74,09	-26	0000
March 21	Fri.	83,35	5	74,10	-29	0000
March 22	Sat.	83,41	6	74,13	-29	0000
March 23	Sun.	83,41	0	74,50	-22	0100
March 24	Mon.	83,44	3	73,48	-30	1000
March 25	Tues.	83,50	6	73,46	-32	1000
March 26	Wed.	83,51	1	73,52	-31	0100
March 27	Thurs.	83,59	8	74,20	-33	0001
March 28	Fri.	83,59	0	74,02	-25	0110
March 29	Sat.	83,59	0	74,02	-28	0010
March 30	Sun.	84,02	3	74,01	-35	0000
March 30–Changeover						
March 31	Mon.	84,03	1	74,02	-30	0000
April 1	Tues.	84,12	9	74,09	-29	0000
April 2	Wed.	84,18	6	74,14	-29	0000
April 3	Thurs.	84,25	7	74,07	-34	0000
April 4	Fri.	84,31	6	74,16	-35	1000
April 5	Sat.	84,37	6	73,58	-32	0000
April 6	Sun.	84,45	8	74,03	-35	0000
April 7	Mon.	84,52	7	74,49	-27	0000
April 8	Tues.	85,00	8	74,08	-30	0000
April 9	Wed.	85,07	7	74,19	-25	0000
April 10	Thurs.	85,11	4	74,24	-25	0001
April 11	Fri.	85,10	-1	74,29	-20	0001
April 12–Changeover						
April 12	Sat.	85,17	7	73,21	-20	0000
April 13	Sun.	85,24	7	73,26	-18	0000
April 14	Mon.	85,30	6	73,52	-25	0000
April 15	Tues.	85,37	7	73,49	-25	0000
April 16	Wed.	85,45	8	73,50	-22	0000

Date		Latitude	Distance Gained N.	Longitude	Evening Temperature °C	Argos Code *
April 17	Thurs.	85,54	9	73,46	-22	0000
April 18	Fri.	86,02	8	73,40	-23	0000
April 19	Sat.	86,07	5	72,13	-24	1000
April 20	Sun.	86,07	0	68,54	-18	0100
April 21	Mon.	86,10	3	67,59	-9	0100
April 22	Tues.	86,12	2	67,09	-16	1000
April 23	Wed.	86,18	6	66,00	-15	0000
April 24	Thurs.	86,18	0	65,08	-15	0000
April 25	Fri.	86,15	-3	62,23	-14	0100
April 26	Sat.	86,18	3	61,41	-13	1000
April 27	Sun.	86,21	3	61,28	-11	1000
April 28	Mon.	86,21	0	61,22	-12	0001
April 28–Changeover						
April 29	Tues.	86,30	9	62,15	-16	0000
April 30	Wed.	86,37	7	62,42	-12	0000
May 1	Thurs.	86,45	8	63,45	-11	0000
May 2	Fri.	86,52	7	65,10	-13	0000
May 3	Sat.	86,57	5	66,52	-11	1000
May 4	Sun.	87,05	8	68,39	-16	0000
May 5	Mon.	87,13	8	71,39	-9	0000
May 6	Tues.	87,22	9	74,35	-5	0000
May 7	Wed.	87,29	7	76,19	-8	1000
May 8	Thurs.	87,39	10	76,55	-2	0000
May 9	Fri.	87,46	7	76,37	-3	0000
May 10	Sat.	87,52	6	75,29	-6	0100
May 11	Sun.	87,57	5	74,13	-9	1000
May 12	Mon.	88,07	10	75,14	-14	0000
May 13	Tues.	88,11	3	75,24	-10	0001
May 14	Wed.	88,10	-1	75,31	-5	0001
May 15	Thurs.	88,10	0	76,39	-2	0110
May 16	Fri.	88,11	1	76,08	-3	0001
May 17–Changeover						
May 17	Sat.	88,20	9	75,26	-6	0000
May 18	Sun.	88,28	8	74,48	-10	0100
May 19	Mon.	88,41	13	75,23	-4	0000
May 20	Tues.	88,53	12	75,34	-2.4	0000
May 21	Wed.	89,02	9	72,39	-2.3	0000
May 22	Thurs.	89,11	9	74,54	-10	0000
May 23	Fri.	89,19	8	72,32	-10	0000
May 24	Sat.	89,28	9	75,29	-7.5	0000
May 25	Sun.	89,44	16	73,15	-7	0000
May 26	Mon.	90,00	16	00,00	-5	0000

*ARGOS CODES

0	0000	Conditions OK, going well
1	1000	Conditions poor, slow going
2	0100	Halted by bad weather, bad ice or open water
3	1100	Radio out of commission, no further radio comms possible
4	0010	Weather poor, resupply/changeover not possible
5	1010	Overcast, visibility good, strip marked, land on lead
6	0110	Overcast, visibility good, strip marked, land on multi-year ice
7	1110	Conditions changed, delay flight, await instructions
8	0001	Conditions excellent; good for changeover
9	1001	Resupply needed ASAP
10	0101	Need medic on evacuation plane, await further instructions
11	1101	Need to evacuate a guide; not urgent
12	0011	Need to evacuate a guide, ASAP
13	1011	Need to evacuate four or less people; not urgent
14	0111	Need to evacuate four or less people, ASAP
15	1111	Need to evacuate whole group ASAP

Numbers 0–3 were for general information and not to be acted on
Numbers 4–8 were information to give to pilots
Numbers 9–15 were requests for changeover, resupply and evacuations

Appendix 5

MENU

Day 1	g	cal	Day 2	g	cal
Breakfast					
Hot Crunchy	100	450	Hot Crunchy	100	450
Powd. Milk	28	100	Powd. Milk	28	100
Butter	56	407	Butter	56	407
	184	957		184	957
Lunch & Snacks					
Salami	112	540	Salami	112	540
Chocolate	100	550	Chocolate	100	550
Peanuts	50	275	Peanuts	50	275
Dried Fruit	50	150	--	--	----
	312	1515		262	1365
Dinner					
Stroganoff	120	445	Bountiful Pasta	123	481
Dried Beef	14	137	Dried Chicken	14	144
Butter	56	407	Powd Shortening	50	455
Cheese	28	115	Cheese	50	205
	218	1104		237	1285
Dessert					
Shortbread	50	250	Shortbread	50	250
Drinks					
Juice Crystals	50	480	Juice Crystals	50	480
Hot Chocolate	60	240	Hot Chocolate	60	240
Tea w/sugar	40	135	Tea w/sugar	40	135
Coffee w/sugar	33	115	Coffee w/sugar	33	115
	183	970		183	970
Total:	947	4796	Total:	916	4827

Day 3	g	cal	Day 4	g	cal
Breakfast					
Hot Crunchy	100	450	Hot Crunchy	100	450
Powd. Milk	28	100	Powd. Milk	28	100
Butter	56	407	Butter	56	407
	184	957		184	957
Lunch & Snacks					
Salami	112	540	Salami	112	540
Chocolate	100	550	Chocolate	100	550
Peanuts	50	275	Peanuts	50	275
Dried Fruit	50	150	Dried Fruit	50	150
	312	1515		312	1515

Dinner	g	cal			g	cal
Oriental S. & S.	155	554		Alfredo Pasta	108	454
Dried Turkey	14	133		Dried Chicken	14	144
Butter	56	407		Powd Shortening	50	455
	--	----		Cheese	25	100
	225	1094			197	1153
Dessert						
Shortbread	50	250		Shortbread	50	250
Drinks						
Juice Crystals	50	480		Juice Crystals	50	480
Hot Chocolate	60	240		Hot Chocolate	60	240
Tea w/sugar	40	135		Tea w/sugar	40	135
Coffee w/sugar	33	115		Coffee w/sugar	33	115
	183	970			183	970
Total:	954	4786		Total:	926	4845

Day 5	g	cal
Breakfast		
Hot Crunchy	100	450
Powd. Milk	28	100
Butter	56	407
	184	957
Lunch & Snacks		
Salami	112	540
Chocolate	100	550
Peanuts	50	275
Dried Fruit	50	150
	312	1515
Dinner		
Big Bill's Bean	124	425
Dried Beef	15	151
Butter	56	407
Parmesan	28	130
	223	1113
Dessert		
Shortbread	50	250
Drinks		
Juice Crystals	50	480
Hot Chocolate	60	240
Tea w/sugar	40	135
Coffee w/sugar	33	115
	183	970
Total:	952	4805

Appendix 6

EQUIPMENT AND CLOTHING

Item	Manufactured by
Pulk (1.6 meter long)	Snow Sled
Harness	Snow Sled
Trace	Custom made
Carabiner	Mountain Equipment Coop (MEC)
Skis	Fisher 99 Crown
Ski poles	Swix Traditional
Ski skins	Montanyl
Ski bindings	UniFlex and Sherpa Berwin
Sleeping system:	
Down sleeping bag	Stephenson Warmlite
Over bag	MEC Gossling
Vapor barrier liner	MEC
Sleeping pad–10cm evazote	MEC
Personal Kit:	
Water bottles x 2	Nalgene
Water bottle jackets x 2	MEC
Plastic bowl, mug, spoon	MEC
Group Equipment:	
Weber tent	Custom made by Richard Weber and Josee Auclair
Shovels x 2	Voile
Ice screws x 6 (titanium)	Irbis
Ice ax	Simond
Snow Saw	Life-Link
Stoves and Cooking:	
Whisperlight shaker	Mountain Safety Research
Fuel bottle (1 liter)	Mountain Safety Research
Stove base	Custom made
Stove fuel	Coleman White Gas (3 liters per day)
Pots x 2	MEC
Coffee pot	MEC
Large spoon	Outdoor Research
Pot scrubby	
Wooden matches & lighters	

Communication:
HF radio   Custom made by Flo Howell
Argos   Custom made by Flo Howell
Personal Locator Beacon   MPR Satfind-406
Spare batteries

Navigation:
GPS x 2   Garmin 45 XL
Compass x 2   Suunto and Silva
Watches x 2   Casio

Safety Equipment:
First aid kit   Custom made
Gun & ammunition   Winchester Model 70, 30-0-6
Throw line rescue bag   Custom made by Matty
Emergency clothing
(spare boot liners, one piece suit)

Other Group Items:
Video camera (Digital)   Panasonic
Tape recorder   Panasonic
Group journal   -
Tent lamp   Coleman
Head lamp   Petzl - Arctic
Thermometer   Taylor Instruments
Anemometer   Wind Wizard
Repair kit   Custom made

Matty's Personal Clothing List

Body:
–one-piece long underwear, capeline	Patagonia
–one-piece pile underwear	Helly Hansen
–one-piece snow suit, micro-fiber	Custom made by Vander
–wind parka w/ black bear fur ruff	Helly Hansen, (used on relay 1–4)
–wind cheater, waterproof/breathable	Vander, (used on relay 5)
–warm-up pants w/ full side zips	Sierra Designs (used only on relay 1 and 2)
–expedition down parka	MEC (used only on relay 1 and 2)
-nylon shelled pile jacket	Patagonia

Feet:
–sock liners	Helly Hansen
–VBL socks	Stephenson
–pile socks, 2 pr.–size 7 and 9	Helly Hansen

Hands:
–polypropylene glove liners, 2 pr.	Helly Hansen
–VBL glove liner	Stephenson (used on relay 1 and 2)
–mittens, nylon shelled pile, 2 pr.	Helly Hansen
–caribou mittens	Inuit made (used on relay 1 and 2)
–cross-country ski leather gloves	Paris (used on relay 4 and 5)
–pile wristlets	Custom made by Matty

Head:
–cowl	Helly Hansen
–neck warmer x 2	Custom made by Matty
–goggles w/nose guard x 2	Cebe
–sunglasses	Cebe (used on relay 4 and 5)

Other:
Toiletries (toothbrush and paste, hair brush, vitamins, sunscreen, nail clippers)
Camera, SLR 35 mm	Canon EOS w/Tamron lens
Advantix camera	Kodak (used on relay 1–3)
Camera, compact 35 mm	Yashica T-4 Super (used on relay 4–5)
Film (8–10 rolls per relay)	Kodak and Fuji film
Personal journal and pencil	